MW00387437

RICHARD TRACY WITH JOHN MORRIS

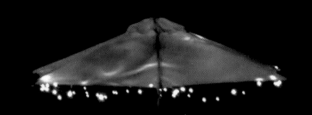

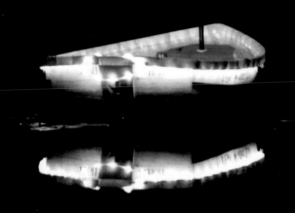

Troll Knoll
A GARDEN LIKE NO OTHER

Copyright © 2016 by Richard Tracy with John Morris. 728009
Library of Congress Control Number: 2016905088

ISBN: Softcover   978-1-5144-8010-6
        Hardcover   978-1-5144-8011-3
        EBook   978-1-5144-8009-0

Printed in the United States of America

Rev. date: 10/24/2016

To order additional copies of this book, contact:
Xlibris
1-888-795-4274
www.Xlibris.com
Orders@Xlibris.com

It takes a village to create a book like this. And there are those without whose inspiration and guidance it would never have happened. Topping that list is Ann Morris.

Without her, there would have been no need for the garden at Troll Knoll. And minus her persistence, encouragement and love, the home and garden could not endure.

Further endowing the continued expansion of Troll Knoll have been some significant contributors: Sebastian Rapport for computer help; Merle Kennealy for bringing folks; Judy Beaver for creative ideas; Eric Sparks for overseeing electronics and surveillance cameras and Sherron Egner for comments and criticism. Certainly not to be forgotten are beloved benefactors from the past such as my mother-in-law, Helen Wilson, who showed me how to frame a view, and my parents, Toxey and Dorothy Morris, who let me fly and told me what I was doing was "fantastic."

Notable contributions came from the family of my collaborator in the enthusiasm and support of his wife, Felicia Tracy and the remarkable proofreading skills of his son Ryan Tracy.

Finally, we owe thanks to the thousands of guests who have followed the troll through the garden. We've never charged admission, but were paid handsomely with observations and suggestions that have added to the fun and adventure of the endeavor.

John Morris

What's Inside

Contents

The English Garden Walk

Introduction

Welcome to Troll Knoll

Chances are you've turned the pages of this book several times before checking out this introduction.

Don't feel sheepish. I've done the same thing many times when reviewing books in my professional capacity as a garden newspaper editor.

But now that you're here, allow me to make some observations.

When I was writing about gardening for the *Sacramento Bee*, a career that stretched over thirty years, I had the extreme pleasure of visiting gardens near and far.

In those glory days, when newspapers were knocking down a handsome profit margin, I was *urged* to travel. Attending symposiums of the Garden Writers Association, for example, brought me to gardens all over the country and Canada.

And as a garden luminary, it was my pleasure to guest-host trips to England, Wales, Scotland, Ireland, France, Italy, Spain, the Netherlands, and New Zealand.

Over those years, I developed a test for a world-class garden. In such a place, you can plant your feet and quietly look around and see that the gardener has placed stones and other landscape objects in a particular manner and created a schedule of blooms to carry beauty through the year. Aspects of the garden that look as if they just happened have been carefully planned, as have the methods of irrigation and lighting pathways.

I share that information in order to explain that I have never seen a garden quite like Troll Knoll. True, it's not Versailles, Villandry, Stourhead, or Giverny. Yet it is a world-class garden in every respect.

First, we will turn all the flowers blue, then turn the alligators to stone . . .

In fact, it's a love story told with tenderness and humor as much as it is a horticultural showcase. That's why, after first visiting in 2004, I urged John Morris, "You have to share this."

He did, and visitors arrived by the tens of thousands. One day, for example, there were seven coaches of California Garden Club members roaming the garden with guidance from the Troll.

And when I suggested that he should write a book about the garden, John drew a deep breath and said, "I love to talk, but I hate to type."

Raising my hand, I said, "I can type." And the die was cast.

We'd usually meet on Wednesday mornings, pick a subject to discuss while my tape recorder rolled, then visit various parts of the garden.

Even after dozens of such visits, I invariably found something in the garden I hadn't noticed before.

John and Ann Morris

And each conversation with John and Ann revealed that every aspect of the landscape is intertwined with the stories of their lives: joy and sorrow, happiness and despair.

I recall one morning when we were seated on the living room sofa with the Morrises' boxers, Pepper and Plato, curled at our feet; and Ann walked in, pausing on her way to the bedroom to change clothes. Arms held out like a scarecrow, she was laughing hysterically, wearing a completely soaked T-shirt.

Obviously, something unexpected had happened on her rounds to see that all the drip emitters and sprinklers were working properly. It was an experience only a true gardener would find humorous.

What about the future of Troll Knoll? John, turning seventy with the publication of the book, oftentimes talks of the new people who will someday own the property. (It's highly unlikely either of the grown Morris children will continue their parents' garden legacy.)

"When gardeners die," John says with a sigh, staring out at the rose garden, "their gardens usually die with them."

If that's the fate of Troll Knoll, at least it's served its purpose for now.

Keep in mind that *garten* in German means "sanctuary," and that's what John was seeking. "Initially, I just wanted a place to take evening walks with Ann."

This book is an opportunity to share that stroll.

Some places to stroll

Ranunculus volans tumulorum or something

Chapter 1

Meet the Troll

Ask anyone who's been on a guided tour of Troll Knoll for their impressions, and they'll most likely laugh and tell of John Morris's lilting Southern accent and add, "It was hard to figure out whether he was telling the truth or pulling our legs!"

And such remarks gladden the heart of the Troll, who insists the purpose of the garden is to have *fun*.

A gift of the golden tongue has been with John since grade school, when, at the age of sixteen, he won prestigious state and national awards for extemporaneous speaking.

Recalling his early education, John says he applied from high school to a number of top-quality colleges, including Yale and Harvard, and was accepted—with a scholarship—at nearly all of them, including Harvard.

An instructor at his high school found this so incredible ("People from Mississippi *aren't* accepted at Ivy League schools!") he telephoned—in front of John and his friends—the Harvard admissions office and was told that John was, indeed, their number one pick.

John explains that this was one of a series of things that happened early on in his career, "where I was trying to do things that weren't necessarily 'inside the box.'"

Smiling wryly, he recalls taking an examination in high school and finishing it far faster than his classmates. So he sat back in his desk and began counting the holes in the ceiling—for which he was suspended from school.

Occasionally, he wore slippers to school and was forced to wear shoes and conform.

A speech contest, where he talked about Communism being taught in the high school, caught the attention of the local news media and was printed—to the consternation of school officials.

At Harvard, he majored in economics for two years before being convinced by his family to study medicine.

The Troll working on the trestle

He completed the pre-med course in *one year* and pursued his degree at the University of Alabama (since Harvard had no medical school openings until the following year).

"I didn't like medical school much," he says with a shrug, "so I went back to Harvard."

"That summer, I met a young lady from Berkeley, California. She generally saw my attitude as eminently reasonable. We dated for a while, then went our separate ways. She returned to Berkeley. Six years later, she sent me a Christmas card. We were married six months later."

He and Ann have been married for more than forty years.

Attaining a degree in economics taught him how to use statistical analysis and mathematics. So how does that apply to the garden at Troll Knoll?

"Our ability is to manage things in an efficient manner," John says nodding. "Except for special projects, we can take care of a twenty-acre garden by ourselves. And that was always our intention. The way to live a life is not to use up the resources you have but to use them as effectively as possible. For example, when there were wooden posts left over from the vineyard, they were painted and used as decorations throughout the garden."

How he wound up in law school at the University of Mississippi is another somewhat convoluted tale.

"We had a neighbor, an attorney whom my father greatly admired," John chuckles, "and almost every time we drove by his house, my father said, 'There's a lawyer with *flair*!'"

And he was called upon when John's misadventures with high school administrators had him on suspension and, therefore, unable to apply for a college scholarship.

"My father told our friend the story, and he pushed back from his desk and drove to the school. In a few hours, I was reinstated."

That ability to right a wrong made a powerful impression. As did his father's pronouncement, "It doesn't matter *what* you do . . . just be the *best* you can be at it."

John ended up attending law school in 1967 at Ole Miss but was drafted and went into the Air Force Reserve before graduation and never went back to the campus for study, instead completing his degree from his parental home in Hattiesburg, Mississippi.

Practicing law with an elderly trial attorney taught him the ropes as well as his own limitations. "Speaking was easy," he says with a smile. "Writing was not. All my life that's been an issue."

And there were other confining issues: "I wanted to *help* people, but it got to where I had to practically ask permission to go to the bathroom. They'd hand me a file for a case to try, and I'd have to insist I meet with the client beforehand. It became impossible.

"One case was about a stroke victim who was held as a virtual prisoner in his own home while his wills were changed over and over, cutting his family out of the assets. My law partner turned the case down because it was not a remunerative case. I didn't know that and accepted it. And that was our first million-dollar case. So in about four years, we went from a law firm of two people and one secretary to a firm with many others and tremendous support.

"Then success became a problem," he observes, "because what you became was a supervisor for a lot of employees, and that was not my thing.

"I had a good practice, and it became fashionable for young lawyers to try a case against me. That became unfair to my clients. Then I was bitten by a mosquito in Mexico, contracted viral meningitis, and as a result of diminished hearing, I couldn't hear what people were saying when giving testimony, so I thought it was time to stop."

Undaunted, he dove into property management and (with Ann's guidance) opened a series of businesses (including a bookstore chain, Pandora's, and an office supply, Copycat). Then he took over a construction firm and was so overwhelmed by the size of losses that could be incurred he went back to vocational/technical night school for five years to learn all there was to know about construction.

"When I retired, at forty-six years of age, I had never built anything for *us*," John said nodding. "Our home here was the first project. I had a contractor hired by the hour, so I'd fly in from Mississippi and had a trailer on the property to stay in while overseeing construction.

"When I bought the property in Penn Valley (burned over by the 49'er fire which started on 9/11 of 1988), Ann went out to look it over and said it was wonderful for its magnificent views. It took me a year to design the house. I did it first as a cardboard model, deciding to make it one-room deep for ample sunlight, then turned it over to an architect to draw plans. I was from a world of square houses, while Ann wanted to take full advantage of the views. She was absolutely right. She also changed the hallway from six to eight feet wide, so a person could better appreciate the art on the walls.

"Our original architect had a very creative bent but wasn't very good at mathematics in our opinion. Ann (who is a UC Berkeley-educated economist) picked that up from the numbers side. Then I finished the work because the contractor left under cover of darkness. I would pay him for the subcontractors he had hired, but sometimes it would be weeks before he'd pay them. Taking over the construction wasn't a problem to me, except I had not planned on it."

The house has four roofs, with vent space between them, and its walls are sixteen inches thick. The floor is four feet thick, with a base layer and an upper one with in-floor heating. It's pinioned and divided into fifteen-foot sections, so it can move back and forth in earthquakes. The only tremor the Morrises recall was several years ago, and it only cracked the concrete on the surrounding High Heel Walk in two places.

Insofar as the planning for irrigating the garden, some twenty miles of PVC pipe and four miles of drip irrigation tubing were employed. It took three days to trench the property on eighty-foot squares.

"Nobody in their right mind would do that," John says laughing, "and I made a colossal blunder in the design so that, at one point, the pipes were in a trench that became forty feet deep after fill was used to change the ground level! The pipes were never designed for that. And what happens if one breaks?"

Pontifications abound at Annsville's speaker lectern

Now every group that goes through the garden follows the silk top-hatted Troll using a speaker phone to tell of such mysteries as the Roman ruins left by Opius VI, the UFO garden, the dinosaurs, Pinky's Trailer Park, and of mischief by the Rinkydinks who roam the knoll.

"I talk about the garden," John concludes, "and what everything means. It's like looking at a picture in a book with a notation to the side. But I'm prone to give a chapter, not just a notation."

Editor's note:

An avowed fan of my writing style, John cringed when I presented my first draft:

"From reading about what I said about me, I find a lot of it irrelevant, even to me. What I intend to say is that a series of experiences in my early childhood and a number of events in my adult life formed the person that I am and what I do now. It probably is not good copy. Many things that I got to do were because my parents were so willing to let me fly. And for the most part, they could help."

He tells of being bullied in grade school for his ability to get high grades:

"I was an instant freak and remained one for the rest of my secondary education days. Being smart is like being tall or short or—it does have its downside. And look at the statistics of what happens to such folks. And I left the 'mind' groups because they were trying so hard to be smart that to me they missed the point. I would like to stick to being a gardener."

A coven meeting for a tour in the garden

The team rolling the paths

Ann Morris and a friend

Chapter 2

Meet Lady Whackemback

Unlike her flamboyant husband, the Troll, Ann Morris is happy to stand quietly on the sidelines when the garden is crawling with visitors. "Something it took time to get used to," she acknowledges.

In fact, a casual visitor watching her trace the sound of laughter from the Troll-guided tour might think she's a guest who wandered onto the wrong path and is looking to rejoin the group. But she's as much a part of its creation and care as John, and her love of gardening is just as deep-seated. The Whackemback name comes from the couple's routine control of weeds along the pathways.

"My mother was an ardent gardener," Ann explains of her role, "and although she made her living as an art teacher, she once told me she wished she had studied landscape architecture instead of art.

"She had an acre of land that had once been an orchard, and there were a lot of trees around it. And it was her goal to look out of every window of the house and see a picture.

"Frankly, although I lived there for most of my growing-up years, I wasn't much interested in gardening. I'd hand-water some things, but that was about it.

"But John had worked with landscaping and gardening from the time he was very young and was very involved with it.

"And after eighteen years of marriage in Mississippi then moving here, I was finally ready to get up to speed. And that's when I enrolled in the UC Master Gardener program and horticulture classes at Sierra College. And the result of that was if I didn't know something about gardening, I knew where to find the answers."

But Ann was aware there were certain limitations to her gardening skills. Primarily, she was unable to visualize what a garden would look like.

"My mother visited here and, right away, was discussing where plants should go and what problems might arise as they matured. I don't have that capability. John does.

"I spend a lot of time with what I call aftercare and keep an eye on plants that might not be getting enough water or too much sun or shade.

"An example would be when John was working on a tapestry of colors near the western side of the house and came across some Chinese fringe plants (*Loropetalum chinensis*) with bright red foliage that he'd planted last fall but had forgotten about.

"Then he came in one day and said that every one of them had died. I marched out there and found two in poor condition and one nearly dead. So I got some water and started making plans to mulch and save them. We've learned through experience that if you put in a little plant, it takes about three years before it's able to maintain itself. Then you can do all the pruning and shaping and turn your attention to younger plants.

"I like the detail things," she says with a smile (perhaps a spin-off of her career as a certified public accountant, during which she served as chief financial officer of a major California hospital system).

Because of the size of the garden at Troll Knoll, the Morrises rely a lot on chemicals, and this is where Ann's attention to detail comes into play.

"I know most chemicals have a shelf life of about five years, so I do a lot of price shopping to determine how much to buy, and because I'm likely to forget mixing quantities, I keep a notebook that tells me how much chemical to use in our sixty-five-gallon sprayer and when to apply fertilizer. I like to do that.

Lots of starts

"And the greatest amount of time in summer is spent on irrigation. I didn't design and install it. John did, initially installing twenty miles of PVC pipe and four miles of drip tubing, and we run all our pumps off solar power, so there are timers on everything, and I see that they're running at the proper time. Water pressure is always a problem, so we have to ensure things are balanced. In early summer, we're running them just over ten hours a day.

"And I plan watering for individual areas. We won't water the lawns at night, for example, because that would create mildew. We have clay soil and have learned that it's better to stagger the watering schedule instead of trying to pour it on all at one time. And you have to keep an eye on sprinklers and drip outlets to see they're working properly."

Now in retirement, except for completing tax return forms for longtime clients, Ann turns her attention to the garden and to coping with the whims of a husband who has boundless imagination.

"We've been married for over forty years," she says, smiling, "and early in our marriage, when I thought I had a better idea for something he was doing, I'd tell him he was crazy. I've now learned he has much more creative ability than I do.

Counting the starts

"But he's encouraged me to stick to my guns. He says, 'When you jump in a river, you have to swim to the other side—not turn around halfway there.'

"But I can't forget about the old house we lived in when we were newlyweds. I decided to replace the carpet and put new charcoal slate on the kitchen floor."

Laughing so hard she has to pause and catch her breath, Ann shakes her head. "Those were expensive mistakes. I picked a shag carpet that needed constant attention, and the dark slate in the kitchen showed every spill.

Our tomatoes for lunch

"So after that I decided interior decorating was not my strength. John's responsible for the décor here at Troll Knoll. And it was tough. We had things from Mississippi that were ours. Then a few years later, we had things from my parents' house and then from *his* parent's house. He combined them into one to make it meld together."

One addition to Troll Knoll was made without Ann's knowledge.

John picked one corner of the property out of sight from the house to create a mock Western town he named Annsville as a surprise birthday present. It has a two-story hotel (which serves as a guest house) and other outbuildings in addition to a mine with an ore cart. It also serves as a wine cellar.

Ann shares her reaction: "I was truly surprised. In those days, I was still working full-time and left in the dark of early morning and returned at night. Even when I look back now, I'm still amazed."

27

Asked if she has a favorite part of the garden, Ann brightens up, saying, "Probably because John is so good at the ornamentals, it's the food part. The orchard was started in the late '90s, and there was a lot of trouble with deer and other things, but eventually, the trees came along, and I enjoy going out and pruning them to keep them short and then harvesting the fruit for our use. I do the same thing with vegetables."

Socrates the Cat

John takes delight in successfully growing plants like palms and oranges that reportedly won't do well in Penn Valley. Similarly, Ann has taken on the challenge of growing blueberries.

"Last year, John brought home a dozen blueberry bushes, very excited about the whole idea of having them, even though we'd tried growing them before and it was a disaster. This time, though, I relied on the Master Gardeners for information and realized they need very, very acidic soil.

"I know pretty much what the soil pH is because I've tested all over the yard, and we do have acid soil. But blueberries like extra things like pine needle mulch and sulfur along with acid fertilizer. And they need ample water, which is supplied every night by drip irrigation."

Another aspect of the garden that Ann particularly enjoys is propagating from cuttings. "The Nevada County UC Master Gardeners' major fund-raiser is a plant sale, and when I was an active member, I used to grow things for that function. I still enjoy it, and John really hasn't got the patience to wait for the cuttings to grow."

Initially, the Morrises raised-bed vegetable garden was located in a very hot and dry part of the property, but they found the water supply there was unreliable, and it was moved to a more hospitable location.

Along with failures, the Morrises found that success can have its drawbacks as well. With all the large windows in their home providing views of the valley and the sierra, the ornamentals thriving near their home were creating a green wall.

Trees were pruned up, and ornamentals were brought back under control through trimming or even removal. The same treatment was given to the several ponds on the property which were becoming too bushy.

But one aspect of growing success is truly appreciated. "When we moved here twenty years ago," Ann says nodding, "there was just no shade at all. It was just plain hot. All day. All month. Lately, we've been commenting on how the shade has created a whole new atmosphere."

Ann takes secret pleasure in walking barefoot along the three-quarter-mile-long paved High Heel Walk that encircles one level of the garden, and she and John routinely take strolls around sunset. "Oh yes," she says smiling, "we take our walks and make mental notes about things that need doing. It's so pretty at that time of day!"

Lady Wackemback in respose

On the veranda porch

Ann at Pond Won in Snow

Chapter 3

Troll House

Most visitors to Troll Knoll never see the inside of Troll House, although it has been on home tours from time to time. The décor, largely John's design, is a tasteful blend of art and artifacts that reflect the spirit of Christmas.

Like the garden, it's elaborately designed and unique. For one thing, it's made of concrete, with sixteen-inch thick walls.

The reason for that, John explains is "I don't want to lose another home to fire."

That's what happened to the Morrises frame home in Hattiesburg, Mississippi. That event, coupled with the passing of John's father and Ann's desire to return to the West, brought them to California.

When asked to describe how the house came to be, John laughs as he says, "There's enough information for another book."

In brief, instead of starting out on an architect's drawing board, the concept for the home began by cutting out a scale model cardboard silhouette of the home's exterior.

"It had rather detailed information on room size and amenities," John explains. "It had to be on one level, one room wide, allowing plenty of light from both sides and providing plenty of vistas."

In fact, there was so much glass that it exceeded limits set by the county building code, and a fine was levied. Ironically, not long afterward, the home won an award from a local utility for its use of structure and glass.

"We used that model to determine how the house would be oriented on the knoll to shut out the blazing summer sun and allow in the winter light," John explains, "and the use of that model was one of the best things we did in planning the House of No Gremlins here."

But despite their best efforts, there were "gremlins" that popped up, such as having to tear out windows on one side of the house and lower them eighteen inches so the garden could be better seen by people seated inside.

Above: House model done before construction

Pausing for a moment to gather his thoughts, John continues, "The window frame extended vistas of the garden, and they're everywhere, even in our oversized walk-in bedroom closet."

And by looking at the floor plan in the cutout, Ann determined that a six-foot-wide hallway from the bedroom to the kitchen wasn't wide enough for people to appreciate the art on the walls. And so the hallway was expanded to eight feet.

More details fell into place, such as twenty-foot structured ceilings, granite windowsills and countertops, and no curtains anywhere. In addition, the home has an expansive attic.

A year after starting the model, it was turned over to an architect to be translated into blueprints to begin construction.

Smiling and nodding, John admits, "This home is built from scratch. You do need some scratch to build such a structure."

Living Room With Model Airplanes.

The dining room overlooks the kitchen garden

Liberal Use Of Glass Brings The Kitchen Garden Indoors

The bedroom windows look out into the garden and the view of the Coastal Mountain Range and the Valley

The Gallery Art Collection

Nike offers a magnificent welcome to Troll Knoll's entrance gardens

Chapter 4

The Garden Entry

When writing for newspapers, one of the most important elements of a story is an opening paragraph called a lede. Usually, it will include as many of the five Ws and the H (who, what, when, where, why, and how) to entice the reader.

In landscaping, the entry to the garden is similar to the lede. And designing the starting point for visitors is enormously important.

"I spent hours sitting in a chair outside in the garden thinking of the entrance," John said nodding, "and didn't really have it completed until seven years after excavating the ponds. It was to be a pathway into the garden.

"As you arrive at the parking area, things have grown up enough that you can barely see there's a house ahead. You're walking up 135-feet of walkway, like ascending the steps of a courthouse, which are deliberately designed that way to tell you you're going somewhere important, and then go to one side of the house to get a glimpse of the statue of *Nike*, which is illuminated in the evening. Then as you move along the paths you see more ornamentation and plantings."

And each plant in the fabric of the design is selected with its long-range impact in mind. A Japanese maple in the atrium was planned as an umbrella canopy, and it took ten years of intensive care to get it to grow as high as the eaves of the roof. John has plans for a liquidambar tree to serve in the same way, and the featured statue of *Winged Venus* has formal plantings to develop a vignette.

Pausing to reflect on the design process, John laughs and says, "I actually planned these things, but as I've told Ann, some of the things I say are terribly corny. But they reveal the passion and feeling of what I want to do. For those who step into the atrium, I want the design to say, 'Welcome to Troll Knoll, our home in a garden.'"

Straight pathways are a rare sight at Troll Knoll. Curved walkways lend an aura of mystery

The viewer's mind asks, "What's beyond the bend?

Chapter 5

Pond Won

The first major vignette that visitors encounter on a tour of Troll Knoll is the pond to the left of Troll House. Their host—dressed in a silk top hat, black leather vest, and tuxedo dress shirt—makes reference to what sounds like "pond one" (there are eight in the garden) but is actually "Pond Won," as in victory over cloudy memories, signified by a stone on its bank etched with the words "Never Give Up."

An untied rowboat, the *Water Lily*, floats silently beneath its colorful umbrella. And sharp-eyed visitors may note that it's festooned with a string of lights powered by a solar battery for evening enchantment.

"The boat appears to know its course and does not even consider the limits of the journey," the Troll explains, "and in perspective, it's one of the many considerations of why we are at home here."

Pond Won, Phase 1

The gravel pathway upon which visitors trod, created to resemble a stream, is the remnant of a long-gone gravel roadway built for dump trucks to haul landfill to the building site, elevating it forty feet.

Pond Won, which has more statuary than any other area of the garden, probably has more personal significance to John Alan Morris than any of the remaining features on the tour.

Those visitors who know of his earlier life in Mississippi assume that the pond is a reflection of his earlier life on the bayou, marginally so.

"I've always pictured living at the edge of the water," John reflects, "and this is it. At one time, returning home to America from Aix en Provence, where we lived for a short while in France, I'd contracted with a boat builder to build a trawler that we'd live on, but the company failed, and it never happened."

John has two poster-sized photographs that help explain his appreciation for the pond. One was taken on a bright autumn day with the water so still it perfectly mirrored the fall color show. Turning it 180 degrees, it's hard to detect which is the foliage and which is the reflection. Only a single leaf floating on the surface of the water offers a clue.

The Water Lily at Night

"There are so many thought processes you can go through with a picture like this," John explains, his voice catching in his throat. "It's like a watercolor, and I did it intentionally because the colors were so striking that particular day, and the water was so calm. I'd taken other pictures earlier in the day, and they looked like it was a different garden."

Another photograph was taken at night, the only light coming from the *Water Lily*'s solar-powered string, which also illuminates the white umbrella. It looks as if the boat were floating in the night sky.

"At night, you really can't see the pond's end," John says nodding. "It's like the *Water Lily* is going off in that direction. So I untie the *Water Lily*, and it does what it wants to. It has motion, and it has life.

"By golly, I'm like this boat," he laughs, slapping a knee. "I appear to know where I'm going, but I have no idea where the limits are."

Pausing for a moment to reflect, John concludes, "In Pond Won, I have my boat, my water, and a drop-dead gorgeous garden I love to work in."

Hey, wait!

One of the bathers at Pond Won

A Fall view of Pond Won that is a favorite

Colors change throughout the year. The fragrance from the many silverberry shrubs greets you to the Pond Won area.

The pergola views the Arboretum, the Vineyard, the Dinosaur Habitat and many other features

George Burns

Cherry Parfait

Chapter 6

The Subject Is Roses

If the only horticultural attraction at Troll Knoll was its rose garden, it would still draw a score of visitors each year.

Edging the curving High Heel Walk for a total of nearly three-quarters of a mile, the roses are what dominate a stunning scene from Troll House windows.

"It's why we had the windows on the back of the house lowered eighteen inches," John says, "so you can comfortably sit in your chair and enjoy the view."

In all, the Morrises estimate there are probably 3,500 roses of all types: hybrid teas, grandifloras, multifloras, tree roses, climbers, and some of the famed David Austin roses. They're the ones that capture the form and fragrance of classic roses, but unlike the old-timers, these rebloom like modern varieties instead of putting on just one show a year.

But wait, you're asking, "How can two retired people prune and care for 3,500 roses?"

Well, consulting rosarians may cringe, but when it's pruning time, John cranks one of his seven-foot extension hedge trimmers and gives them a flat-top haircut. Then Ann comes along with her trusty Felco hand pruners and "picks up the pieces" where necessary, particularly on the hybrid tea or standard roses. The standards, growing bushy heads on long trunks, are particularly prone to damage in heavy winds or rains. For their own protection, they're cut back sharply and look naked in March.

Insofar as fertilization is concerned, Ann heads to the local farm supply store and buys the most economical 15-15-15 balanced fertilizer available.

"I think it was a fellow UC Master Gardener who remarked that plants really don't know the source of food they're getting, and they definitely need nitrogen," she smiles, "so we skipped the fancy formulations.

"After the first flush of bloom in spring, we let them just sit through the heat of July, then begin feeding and cutting in August. It takes about two months. We let the plants rest in January.

"When we first started, we were not very knowledgeable about which roses to plant for disease and insect resistance and were picking some simply because of their romantic names. But the American Rose Society has an excellent booklet that rates the plants by performance, and we never plant anything rated below the upper sevens."

Many modern roses are grafted unto sturdy rootstock, but the Morrises quickly learned that non-grafted carpet roses and shrub roses have better longevity in their location. And they're very highly rated by the Rose Society.

Yes, there are favorites, like John's beloved "Hot Cocoa," and Ann propagated about sixty of them for planting throughout the garden. In total, she's done about 1,600 plants this way.

"When I was taking garden classes at Sierra College," Ann says, "they graded plants by their ability to cope with snow load, and I really didn't know what they meant since I'd never gardened in snow zones. That's not too much of a concern here, but if they get wet in the rain and then high winds come along, they'll break."

An interesting sidelight to the rose garden story is told by John about getting a catalog for David Austin roses and noticing that they offered help by an esteemed garden designer (Michael Marriott) if a person were designing a garden using their roses.

So he e-mailed the dimensions of the garden, asking for a colorful arrangement that could be repeated on the High Heel Walk about three quarters of a mile long, with each area being about 230-feet long and 10-feet deep.

Varieties like Cherry Parfait are along miles of walks

Searching for a better word, communication stuttered for a period; but John persisted, and finally, Marriott said he'd been commissioned to design a governmental planting in Venezuela and would work on it after that was complete.

Marriott faxed a plan that John felt was "absolutely gorgeous" and promptly bought 150 David Austin roses.

"And so I planted them," John says, drawing a deep breath and staring out the window, "and within six months, many of them were dead! Upon studying Marriott's selections, I found that those roses were very good in a climate like San Francisco's. In fact, he'd done the garden at Filoli, on the San Francisco Peninsula.

"It turns out those roses were enjoyed very much by gophers and voles. I could sit here and look at those roses and watch them wiggle as the critters ate the roots. The survivors look good but are also susceptible to black spot, aphids, and every other disease known to mankind. We have enough now, though, that if we lose a few, it just lightens the load at pruning time."

When Edmond's Roses was moving its operation from Oregon to the Midwest, they had a sale the Morrises found attractive and bought some sturdy stock—about 250 plants. In John's words, "It was a very busy month after that."

"But with no extra care, they're now six to eight feet tall with routine water and feeding. The deer help me prune them. And types like "Marilyn Monroe" did extremely well. They're some of the sturdiest roses we have, and I think it's because they were grown at our elevation."

Other plants have been picked out of grocery cart displays outside retail stores, some have come from visits to major suppliers, but they all have one thing in common: "Roses are an exceptional plant here, blooming almost all year, and need only two or three sprayings for mildew in spring. I haven't found another plant for here that has as much splash for as little effort. That's not the general perception."

Careful consideration is given to colors in rose plantings. Most of these are real knockouts

Intermingling vertical accents like Kniphofia and iris to roses on the High Heel Walk vista.

Perennials carefully selected frame the distant vista.

Chapter 7

The Story of Kwan Yin

Of all the pieces of sculpture at Troll Knoll, there is only one from the Asian culture. It's the statue of *Kwan Yin*, the goddess of compassion, whose influence is seen throughout the garden.

"*Kwan Yin* is the only statuary visible from the house," John acknowledges, "both day and night. When she's lit after dark, it's very dramatic with the Japanese lanterns nearby. If there's a breeze, the lanterns seem to be floating, and there are also lights shining through from the statuary angels on the other side of the hedge."

As revered in China, Korea, Japan, and Malaysia as the Virgin Mary as in Christian cultures, Kwan Yin is worshiped for attaining enlightenment, then turning away from the gateway to heaven to return to Earth and aid mankind.

At Troll Knoll, her presence creates an atmosphere of serenity that even affects wild animals.

"One night Ann and I felt as if we were being watched," John recalls, "and we looked out at a table near *Kwan Yin* where we kept fish food and saw it was being eaten by a mama raccoon and five of her babies. They never took their eyes off us while they ate. Normally, I'm upset at the idea of raccoon being near the koi pond, but we really enjoyed watching each other. It was very calm and relaxing.

"Another time the largest wild turkey I've ever seen here was out on our veranda, quietly going from window to window, looking in. There's something about that area that's different."

Acknowledging that aside from his daughter-in-law, he has no direct contact with the Asian culture, John has nonetheless relied heavily on the principles of feng shui in the garden's design. Nancilee Wydra's *Feng Shui in the Garden: Simple Solutions for Creating Comforting, Life-Affirming Gardens of the Soul* has been a guide from the start, using such things as curving pathways to soften its appearance and create a sense of mystery.

The gravel pathway that visitors trod as they begin a garden tour, for example, is designed to resemble a stream. At *Kwan Yin*'s back, a long silverberry (*Eleagnus* sp.) hedge has been pruned to resemble a long mysterious creature with many legs that protects the goddess.

"Children see it right away," John says smiling, "but most adults can't. I guess I'm going to have to make its big eyes more obvious."

And the message of the setting once again pays tribute to the idea of love that pervades throughout the garden.

One of John's favorite passages within Wydra's book is written by Eric Fromm:

"Love is not primarily a relationship to a specific person. It is an attitude, an orientation of character, which determines the relatedness of a person to a whole, not towards one object of love. If I love one person, I love all persons. I love life. I love, through you, the world. I love, in you, also myself."

Kwan Yin provides thoughtful views.

A romantic evening destination

Chapter 8

The Three Graces

As any student of Greek mythology knows, the Three Graces are the daughters of Zeus, representing aspects of charm, beauty, and creativity. But . . . uh . . . their mother was allegedly Aphrodite, not Hera (a.k.a. Mrs. Zeus).

One can only imagine the thunder on Mount Olympus when that little nugget of information came to light.

Be that as it may, at Troll Knoll, the three women (Euphrosyne, Aglaia, and Thalia) are quietly growing green with mold from the fountain that splashes overhead at what has become a significant garden destination both by day and night.

Resting on a foot-thick reinforced concrete pad, the thousand-pound concrete statue occupies an overlook that provides a stunning view of surrounding mountains and a comfortable seating area for contemplation.

"We made seven trips to European gardens and saw how statuary was employed there," John explains, "and learned the mythological love stories. Among the attributes of the Three Graces were the qualities of passion, reflection, and honor. Ann reflects all those ideals, and this garden is for her."

And why are they concrete, instead of granite or marble?

"We had a choice of materials," John says, "and felt concrete was more in keeping with the thirty-five other pieces of statuary in the garden, and it's easier to maintain. If pieces break off over the years, I'll display them as if they broke over the centuries."

"Now, when I see a piece of statuary in a garden," he concludes, "I look at it as being more than just 'pretty.' It keeps your thoughts moving. I've written a catalog of the statuary here, and someday may offer a tour discussing just this aspect of the garden."

The Three Graces is a sunken garden featuring passive solar heating of the benches and a wonderful view to the western valley and Coastal Mountain Range.

It is one of two gardens that were done to honor Lady Whackemback.

The distant view of the Coastal Mountains and Sutter Buttes from the Three Graces

The Three Graces drops lower to have the vista so striking in the distance and from above

The angel Gabriel sounds our entrance to the area

Chapter 9

Statues Become Punctuation

Years ago, on a visit to the magnificent Floriade flower show in the Netherlands, I noticed the incredible bulb garden display (which moves from place to place each year) was staged in an area divided by nature.

And obviously designed to maintain its grandeur, the planners had arranged perhaps two dozen identical copies of the famed *Venus de Milo* statue along each side of a wide pathway crossing the divide.

But one pedestal in the row was empty. And as I watched, one woman after another paused, then mounted the pedestal, and took the opportunity to pose fully clothed, unlike the scantily clad Venus, arms covering strategic parts of the anatomy, while friends took photographs.

Statuary served a distinct purpose there, as it does at Troll Knoll.

"In all, we have thirty-six pieces of large statuary in the garden," John explains, "and we use them as focal points, with enough distance between them that you can pause in that area and think about it before walking on. And you're not inundated with color."

Behind Eve is Troll Knoll's apple orchard

While visiting the splendid gardens of England, John and Ann were charmed by country gardens at places like Anne Hathaway's Cottage but realized that keeping them in bloom on a large scale at Troll Knoll would call for a small army of gardeners.

Spots of color, anchored by the statuary, would have to suffice instead of swaths of color at the famed Butchart Gardens in British Columbia tended by platoons of caretakers.

Another temptation was to establish a stream through the garden, like the ones they saw near Banff and Lake Louise. But a new touch had been added to the intermittent hillside stream: there are serene faces scattered along the stream bed. John cast them himself and plans to have bubbles coming from the mouths of a select few.

Just another touch of whimsy.

"In all, we have thirty-six pieces of large
statuary in the garden," John explains,
"and we use them as focal points,
with enough distance between them
that you can pause in that area and
think about it before walking on."

Some statuary is miniature, such as the tiny representation of Ann within the Wardian case

Chapter 10

A Garden within a Garden

Back in the early 1800s, plant explorers had a devil of a time getting live plants back home because of the beating they took on long sea voyages. Or if they did survive the trip, they perished in the polluted air of cities.

One such London horticulturist was Dr. Nathaniel Bagshaw Ward, who noticed that cocoons of moths he collected had survived for a long time in sealed bottles. In one such flask, he watched a fern grow from a spore that had found a tiny bit of soil.

Curious on the procedure, he had a carpenter build a wooden case with tightly fitted glass, creating what we now call a terrarium and put plants, like orchids, inside. Much to his delight, they thrived.

And so these Wardian cases came into wide use transporting plants and providing safe haven from salty sea air in transit or industrial pollution in cities. They also became intriguing ornaments in the homes and gardens of the wealthy.

"Without them," John observes, "we'd have had no orchids or houseplants prior to air transportation."

At present, the seven Wardian cases, along the High Heel Walk, are from a catalog. Handsome four-foot-tall rectangular metal and glass enclosures, they present striking focal points by day and night. There are some plants inside, in the evening illuminated by solar-powered lights that appear to be substantial white wax candles.

Armed with glass donated by a nursery whose greenhouse was being dismantled, John is formulating plans for building more cases that will contain plants.

Once he does, the task of keeping the plants from cooking in the sun or being overcome with fungi in deep shade becomes Ann's job. Experience has shown that fuzzy-leafed plants don't do well in such environments since their leaves retain moisture.

Troll Knoll's gardens within gardens also include cloches. These large bell-shaped glass jars provide their own environments for plants or miniature landscapes. But caution is urged in reference to where they're located.

"We had one cloche sitting atop a drip irrigation line, and the heat from the reflected sunlight *melted* it," Ann recalls, "and once, we found the surrounding grass smoldering! They have no ventilation. We have them on concrete now."

Chapter 11
The Path of Lesser Significance

does not have the best view

has a few forks in the path

"Never follow the path of lesser significance" was advice John heard years ago from an adviser on how to dress for a successful courtroom appearance.

"I was told to wear a blue suit with a pale blue shirt," John recalls, "and never wear a vest. Plus, if I were to wear a raincoat, it should be black, which commands more attention for me, rather than brown."

And he and a fellow attorney tested these tidbits of wisdom and found them to be both true and effective. Essentially, the message was "Go for it. Give it everything you've got. Win."

In giving a tip of the hat to his long-ago adviser, John created his own Path of Lesser Significance at Troll Knoll for those not so concerned with victory or prominence. And few people who have visited the garden have ever heard of it, aside from seeing a sign along a "more significant" pathway, such as the road to Annsville.

"It's so insignificant I seldom mention it." The Troll smiles. "The path is adjacent to Opius VI's temple and extends from Nowhere Important to the Balustrade Overlook at the Western Meadow. The path does not really go anywhere, certainly does not have the best view as does the overlook and the temple, has a lot of forks, and as a vignette does not mean much. Also, the seating is very small and misplaced."

But in reality, the path (which features signs reading "Does not have the best view" and "Has a few forks in the path" and "For the most part, ends nowhere") took as much planning as many other garden features. During construction, for example, a workman operating an oversized Troy-Bilt Big Red tiller was thrown over its handlebars when it hit a boulder.

Unlike other features of the garden, it is there for the simple purpose of underwhelming the viewer.

A view from the Path of Lesser Significance

Chapter 12

The Mossy Green Path

Once upon a time, an old mansion sat on the crest of what is now Troll Knoll. Its owners had gone to their final reward, and their children lived in far-off lands.

A wildfire that engulfed the tinder-dry structure spelled its future, and that was followed by the unfeeling blades of bulldozers.

All that remained of the glory that was were mossy green paths that once led to the sprawling ornamental garden. But there was no one to appreciate the fluorescent green pathways that winter rains encouraged.

The tale is a myth, conjured up from the fertile imagination of John Alan Morris, but one that he and Ann cherish immeasurably.

When John first mentioned the Mossy Green Path that he'd created using a huge Troy-Bilt "Big Red" tiller, with liberal applications of buttermilk and Miracle-Grow fertilizer to inspire moss growth, I pictured it as being a relatively short one. Instead, it consists of several passageways, the longest meandering through foliage from the Ruins of Opius VI to Annsville, a distance of a better part of a mile.

Few Troll tours venture there nowadays, primarily for safety reasons as fallen pine needles and leaves make for slippery footing. On the last Mossy Green Path tour, John says three participants stumbled—without harm—and that was the final bell for the adventure.

Urging me to watch my step, John began an autumn jaunt, explaining, "For every garden walk here, there's a back path. When we started the garden, I went to landscape architects and got some interesting ideas for pathways. One woman talked to me about 'soilcrete' paths made by mixing cement with soil."

The look that mix created fit perfectly into John's vision of making believe an old home had existed on the knoll, and when it was torn down, the original garden's rugged pathways still remained.

Mossy Green Path at Annsville

"The soilcrete interested me because it looked very, very old," he explains, "and it was ideal in matching the 'ancient' ruins as well as being easy to maintain."

Besides turning a vivid fluorescent green in late fall, the path isn't slippery. "I thought the moss would be slimy in rainy weather," John says, "but it's not. The water goes straight through because it's porous.

"But when I put these soilcrete pathways in, I had no idea how many sacks of cement it might take," he grimaced, eyebrows raised. "Hundreds. Maybe more than a thousand!"

Still, the moss continues to get better, year after year, and the Morrises keep track of its pH level to make sure it's growing properly.

Sights to be seen along the way include a large concrete checkerboard, with a game in progress. It goes unnoticed by those traveling the nearby Old Annsville Road. The same goes for a secondary gold mine shaft, Sea Mia Portal, which John insists is French for, "See my ***!"

"It belongs to a guy who was fired from the Two Dog Mine," John explains with a smile. "So he started mining a new gold vein intersecting the Two Dog."

Nearby, an unpainted wooden storage building looks like a traditional outhouse from the Old West, but it's actually used for storage. And simply because he and Ann decided "we need some more animals," there are several life-sized cast aluminum sheep grazing nearby.

Providing botanical interest, bunch grasses are combined with Shasta daisies because, John explains, "The Annsville cemetery's occupants need to be 'pushing up daisies.'"

The Northern Oasis is an unexpected broad circular patch of green lawn that seems to be thriving near a secret garden that sadly isn't.

"I tried to do a canopy of deciduous trees," John sighs, "but it's too remote and too difficult to work with."

And close to Pinky's Trailer Park, there are small circular polka dots of lawn that can be easily mowed within metal barrel rings.

And although few visitors will be invited to tread the Mossy Green Path, John hopes to someday capture its essence in a quintessential photograph taken by moonlight with a light covering of snow. "I'm just not sure I have the skills to do it," he sighs

In the meantime, he laughs, "If I ever need something extra to do, these paths will provide that opportunity. To us, the Mossy Green Path is one of the most dramatic parts of the garden."

You can pause and reflect on the next move at the checkerboard.

A vista from the mossy green path

Ants' view of the Power of Two

Chapter 13

Ants in the Plants

Maybe it was the childhood experience of watching giant radioactive ants feast on human morsels in the 1954 movie *Them!* that instilled my dislike for the industrious creatures.

Even now, when someone talks of ants, I impulsively brush off my forearms.

And until visiting Troll Knoll, I'd never heard of such a thing as an ant garden.

But neither have the vast majority of visitors who trail John on a guided tour through the garden.

"When I'm taking them down there, I direct their attention to the dinosaurs in the distance," John says with a chuckle, "and all of a sudden, they realize there are these sixteen-to twenty-four-inch metallic ants at their feet, and you hear all kinds of squeals. Then everyone is taking pictures!"

The creatures in question were created from recycled metal by artisans in Southern Mexico, John explains, "and they cost less than just the price of materials if I'd made them myself. I had that in mind after I saw one of them (using smooth, rounded stones for their bodies) in a nursery."

Now there are hundreds of them, some surrounding an emptied Coca-Cola can (as ants are wont to do) and others are trudging uphill in single file from a sand mound.

"That's what gave me the idea," John acknowledges, "I had to find a use for the sand left over from building the sand trap on the golf course. Originally, I was going to call it the Power of One, but Ann saw two very large ants who are obviously interested in each other (they glow at night) and decided a better name was the Power of *Two*. It's become one of the most popular attractions on the property."

The ants have rusted as John hoped they would, but to protect them from further deterioration, he decided to apply a few coats of clear paint.

"So I went to the hardware store and asked the clerk if they had any paint for ants," he laughs. "I love doing things like that."

Ground under repair

Pepper and the Troll discussing gardening with Tri

Chapter 14

The Dinosaur Habitat

A chance remark by a Troll Knoll visitor that an area near the Vineyard Maze "looks like dinosaurs once lived here" planted a seed in John's fertile imagination.

And then one day, while driving toward Marysville, he spotted a house with large fiberglass dinosaurs for sale. The dust hadn't settled on the driveway before he bought a group of five.

"There was a triceratops with two babies," John smiles, "along with a brontosaurus that reminded me of the logo for the old Sinclair Oil Company (immediately named "Sinclair") in addition to a pterodactyl with a twenty-foot wingspan and a fearsome *Tyrannosaurus rex*."

How to stage the prehistoric additions in the garden for best effect took some thinking. The triceratops (with "Tri-baby one" and "Tri-baby two") are eye-catchers from the pathway edging the Ant Garden.

"Then we have the pterodactyl nesting place (large eggs in the crotch of a tree) away from the others. I meant to put it in an area where it might take flight, with restraints, on windy days. But when I was installing it with help, a gust of wind came up, and suddenly, a 150-pound man who was helping me was lifted off his feet. He'd become the base point for a kite. It was one of those moments when I wished I'd had my camera along."

Now Teri is anchored with four-inch steel posts but is still allowed some degree of flight. It was a photograph of John and his Boxer Pepper looking up at the dinosaur that appeared as a teaser on the front page of the *Sacramento Bee* the day a story ran in the *California Life Magazine* that brought over a hundred people to the Morrises' front gate.

"I have no idea how they knew my address," John says, shaking his head, "but they wanted to see the garden."

The attention the dinosaurs got precipitated the creation of the Ant Garden. John justifies, "Because you can't have the dinosaurs hanging out all by themselves.

"I wanted the dinosaurs to have something to munch on," John says. "So I planted some ginkgo trees (a species dating back to prehistoric times), but they didn't take a liking to that area of the garden."

And since Troll Knoll is a happy place, it was important to John that the dinosaurs were smiling. And they are. In the case of the *Tyrannosaurus rex*, of course, it's hard to tell if it's in a good mood or just getting ready for lunch. Partially concealed in foliage along a pathway leading to Annsville, he's often unnoticed by visitors who instinctively step backward when John alerts them of his presence.

"It's what makes the garden special," John concludes with a grin. "You walk around a corner expecting to see one thing and suddenly find something completely unexpected."

Sinclair is a favorite in the Dinosaur Habitat

It is not the dinosaur that you can see that is the problem! The nest is several feet across, and the eggs are as big as basketballs . . . and T. rex *is in the bushes.*

30 for lunch?

Yes, it is a producing vineyard and a maze!

Chapter 15

An A-maze-ing Vineyard

With all the other edible crops growing at Troll Knoll, it made perfect sense to the Morrises that a hillside vineyard be added to the mix. It could fit nicely on a five-acre parcel near the Knoll's parking area.

John attended a viticulture session in 2002 at the University of California at Davis, seeking advice on the project, "And I was told by some of the specialists they'd come up for an on-site inspection if I would be so kind as to supply lunch."

Done deal.

Among the things he learned were that the white wine varieties he and Ann cherish so much don't do well in Troll Knoll's climate, but a number of reds should thrive to make a tasty blend. Keep in mind, the area had been a major wine producer before the Napa Valley growers took prominence, and today there are eighteen wineries in Nevada County.

Another incentive was that installing a vineyard would make an ideal "senior project" for their son, John, in his final year of high school.

Yet another boost was that the Morrises' daughter, Stephanie, had married and was intent upon having children. And John dreamed of making a maze vineyard for them to play in.

"A square maze didn't appeal to me," John explains with one of those classic Troll grins, "so I designed a pie-shaped one but was told it was impractical because building it on a curve would create so much tension on the structure that it would collapse on itself."

In a past project that John was told "couldn't be done," a friend urged him on, saying, "John Alan, that's no mean feat for a high stepper!"

And oh, how he enjoys such challenges, especially when contractors make exorbitant bids on installing the infrastructure.

"I bought an auger, along with some substantial posts, and with the help of two men, had it installed in a single morning," he says, smiling contentedly. "And we did it with posts of varying heights and concrete steps to make walkways. We planted 119 grapevines, six varieties to make a blended wine, with fourteen different types of table grapes for snacks at the seven entrances."

The vineyard, watered by drip irrigation, was producing wine in roughly nine years. And John, a white wine fan, hasn't had a drop of it. ("It's like our nine-hole golf course I never play golf on," he chuckles.)

The maze, which takes John about six minutes to negotiate on a good day, can be changed fairly easily "to present new challenges to our three smarty-pants grandchildren."

But when grandson Simon was seven, he did some one-upsmanship with his grandfather. "I know how to do this," he said and simply walked around the maze perimeter from entrance to exit.

But perhaps the new traffic pattern will slow down the deer that routinely help prune the vines in the maze vineyard and throughout the garden in locations like the Ruins of Opius VI.

A Spring view across the vineyard toward the arboretum

The alley transitions from the Vineyard and Sunken Garden to The Course at Troll Knoll

To the left is the entrance and transition from the Vineyard thru the Sunken Garden to the Course

113

114

Chapter 16

Golf, Anyone?

Why would a family that never plays golf include a challenging nine-hole golf course within its garden?

Well, keep in mind that a prerequisite of any garden element at Troll Knoll is that it has to be fun. It was fun for John Morris to create in an area devoted primarily to being a fire break, and it has been, in John's words, "a hoot!" for numerous guests.

Most notably, the course, which features weedy and overgrown stone steps from the mythical old mansion, has been a source of entertainment for the Morris grandchildren. John routinely changes the numbers on the holes to provide new excitement.

And the Red Hats (a Rabelaisian coven of ladies intent upon whimsy and merriment) have played here as well. John points out the fact that not one of them finished the first-and-only Troll Knoll tournament provides testament to its many challenges.

With its main entrance through the Sunken Garden, the Course of Course is liberally dotted with "Out of Bounds" and "Open for Winter Play" signs but is without grass due to its water consumption and is without a feature found on ordinary golf courses: a sand trap.

Why, you ask?

John replies with one word: "Cats!"

A giant litter box is *not* part of the grand scheme at Troll Knoll. Over the years sand traps have been added nowadays and since this book began, but not without reservation.

Chapter 17

The Boxer Bog

Among the eight ponds at Troll Knoll, the one that gets the most laughs from tour groups is the Boxer Bog adjacent to the Swamp Garden. That's because the resident boxers, Pepper and Plato, take delight in plunging into the water and sending it splashing in every direction.

"The odd thing is, though, that they almost never do that on their own when no one else is around," John testifies. "They just do it for guests!"

But they've made it their own.

Originally, plans were to have a natural pond and waterfall at one end of the swamp, along with a small sand beach. But keeping the water level up was a big problem because of all the crevices in the rock there.

"So we decided to use concrete and sealers like bentonite and gunite," John explained, "but you could still see where water was leaking through. So when our son John was visiting, we decided to install a pond liner.

"Ann had come to witness the event, and with John at one end of the liner and me at the other, I heard her saying 'John . . . John . . .' and thought she was calling to our son. But she was warning me that at least two large rattlesnakes had been aroused by our activity!"

For safety's sake, the concepts of a swimming pool, waterfall, and sandy beach were scuttled. But the liner did prevent any further decline in the water level. And it became a canine playground.

"When Plato was a puppy, he particularly enjoyed romping through the water in the bog," John recalls, "but one day, when I was approaching with Pepper (Plato's dam), I heard him barking. He'd discovered a rattlesnake! Pepper quickly assessed the situation and put herself directly between Plato and the snake and took the strike on a rear leg!

Well, rattlesnakes are one thing. Dinosaurs are another. Ann recalls when the fearsome fiberglass replicas of our prehistoric predecessors were delivered in sections and assembled on the property.

"It took a long time for Pepper to come to terms with them," she says, laughing.

Chapter 18

The Swamp Garden

"You can take a boy out of the swamp, but you can't take the swamp out of a boy."

That fact and John's abiding love for his native Mississippi meant there would be a swamp garden at Troll Knoll. No question about it.

But where?

The perfect site was the forty-foot depression left from digging soil to move atop Troll Knoll and provide a base for Troll House. But here, unlike Mississippi, you can't punch a hole in the ground and watch it fill with water. Rocky crevices let it escape. And our climate really isn't suitable for mosses and cypress trees whose "knees" protrude from the water.

So now what?

John fills in the details on what otherwise is known as Pond Three.

Minstrel frog

"The Mississippi River has a place in my heart," he explains, and just the mention of it makes his Southern dialect become more pronounced. "The river wants to go west in Louisiana. The people do not want it to go there. A bunch of French folks love to live there, mixing it up with the Spanish and Indians. Longfellow wrote a beautiful poem about it.

"Pond Three wants to go west as well, of course. But that is a different story, as I have mentioned. Since Pond Three was an engineering nightmare, a natural swimming hole to the side would be nothing short of a personal nightmare, according to the Mistress of the Manor after seeing two rattlesnakes residing in the area. And she also mentioned that it would be a cool day in a hot place when I found her swimming in that natural swimming hole with local friends.

"So that area became the Boxer Bog, a part of the swamps at Troll Knoll. The view had to be local but needed a viewpoint. The swamps at Troll Knoll, following the footsteps of its great grandfather, the Mississippi, extended past the length of a football field and had no passage across its ever-extending wanderings. As a project to protect the view, the great bridge in the swamp provided a view, was a suitable home for a Troll and became a passage to another life, of course.

"The perspective that sold the project to the development committee is that it provided another vignette called Ann's Answer to Monet, a water lily garden in the swamps."

The moss is there, as are cypress trees, water lilies, reeds, and colorful aquatic plants, along with frogs and reptiles and raccoons. All that's missing is the music of Steven Foster. But if passersby listen closely, they might hear Foster's unforgettable melodies being played by a quartet of musical frogs seated on the far bank.

Ok, ok, if they couldn't grow birds of paradise, why are we here?

Sunset at the Ruins

Chapter 19

Ruins of Opius VI

What can be said about the Ruins of Opius VI? Its stark white columns draped with Concord grape vines are a traffic stopper on garden tours. Pressed for an explanation, John explains in uncharacteristically brief fashion,

"Opius VI is the imaginary Roman ruler in the lands of Troll Knoll. His name is a derivative of Opus, meaning 'for all.' He was from a long line of such, and the temple of Opius VI was built by his loyal servants after the Battle for Troll Knoll. Actually, there have been several battles that it honors. It is part of a greater complex that includes the Three Graces Fountain area and the long curving path and steps to the temple. It was found in the bushes and undergrowth as one of the early discoveries by the property owners. It overlooks the valley to the west, the coastal mountain range, and is the most beautiful when those of interest are within its columns."

But there's more to the story—much more. Remember that every facet of the garden is a conceptual metaphor linked to the Morrises' lives, and this important destination point is a prime example.

The *real* Battle of Troll Knoll occurred one Christmas Eve, when daughter Stephanie came home from school and announced that upon graduation, she was going to get an advanced degree at the University of Kentucky in a subject that offered little to no chance of her making a living.

The Troll bellowed in outrage. His daughter, displaying the courage that Troll families are noted for, bellowed back, "What do you want me to do, become a lawyer?"

When the armies disengaged and the dust of battle had settled, it was agreed that pursuing a law career might not be a bad idea after all. But where would she study? Numerous options were explored, and then the prestigious University of Chicago expressed interest in her studying there at a cost that staggered Lord and Lady Whackemback. Precious relics were put on the market, and Stephanie was catapulted into a successful law career.

The ruins of the temple of Opius VI at night

Meanwhile, the Troll pondered ways of commemorating the struggle and hit upon the idea of erecting a temple honoring Opius VI. That could be done, he learned, at a cost of about $300,000.

Stepping back from such an investment, the Troll decided a ruins would be a significant memorial and would be significantly less expensive if he did the work with the help of a craftsman skilled in the art of steel reinforcing on bridges.

"The next people who live here may decide to tear it down," John says, drawing a deep breath, "but it will take a bulldozer to do it."

Or they might take the fantasy a bit further, glassing it in for various purposes. The location has easy access to power and water, and nighttime visitors are entertained by the adjacent statue of a drunken Bacchus bathed in flashing red light.

"I proposed glassing it in," the Troll says, staring out at the garden, "but the accountant (Lady Whackemback) wouldn't approve it."

The realm of Opius

Chapter 20

Ann's Kitchen Garden

The saying "If only I knew then what I know now" applies to a vast number of things, including growing one's own food.

Standing at the granite-topped center island in her kitchen, dicing vegetables, Ann reminisces, "Twenty-five years ago, before we moved here, to me, a vegetable garden was warm season tomatoes and corn and all that kind of thing. Now the longer we've been up here, I realize there are more things that prefer the cool season. And it's actually a lot easier and a lot more accommodating on the human who has to do it, especially when you're out there in the afternoon in spring and temperatures are heating up and you're in a hurry to get done and get back in the house where it's cool. By mid-October, I'm out there putting in lettuce and all these cool season things and not feeling rushed.

"Like many things we've learned about gardening," Ann says, "if only there was some way we could transfer this knowledge to someone who's younger than we are. You learn through experience.

"I think the most pleasant time in the garden is in fall and winter. When we first moved here, we planted all these fruit trees to make jam, which meant standing over a hot stove in summer. I now realize my preferred harvests are wintertime fruits. Lemons will hang on a tree for months!"

Christmas Lemons

"Here, with a big garden, if you look the other way in summer, you lose your crop. You work all year, and then you've only got about two or three weeks while it's ripe. Then it's gone. Or the deer get it. So it's been an interesting learning experience all along, just as we've learned a lot about ornamentals.

Now Showing

"Twenty-five years ago, if I was going to cook something, I'd look for a recipe and pick out something because it looks good. And now I pick out a recipe because of what's ready to harvest in the garden.

"We spend a lot of time visiting local farmer's markets, not so much to buy things as to see what they've grown. And if they can grow it, so can we!

"Sometimes I get a crop of something, though, and am still not organized about what I'm going to do with it. There's too much for what I know how to do."

Is overproduction a common problem?

"Absolutely. John likes voluminous masses of plants to make a statement. Well, an example is cherry tomatoes. I read, before planting them, they're a bit prolific, and one or two plants are more than enough for a small family. There are just two of us, and I knew we had too many, but he said, 'Oh, but they look pretty!' and a good share wind up on the ground. That happens a lot.

"And sometimes, with favorable weather, even a few plants produce far more than we can use, like the lemon trees. We pick ten to fifteen dozen, and the trees still look like they haven't been touched."

My wife, Felicia, shared samples of marmalade made from Seville oranges (picked from Sacramento street trees) with the Morrises, and Ann enjoyed its tangy bitter flavor.

(The origin of marmalade, according to one story, came from the defeat of the Spanish Armada in 1588, when thousands of the bitter Seville oranges—kept on board to prevent scurvy among the sailors—floated ashore from sunken ships. Thrifty English villagers turned them into a tasty treat.)

"The only marmalade I make," Ann says, "is from our Washington navel oranges. Some recipes are pretty complicated and beyond my patience level. But using this one, you simply cut them up, put them in a food processor, and that's it. But you also need fresh cranberries. And I've discovered that, in this area, fresh cranberries are available at Thanksgiving and maybe Christmas, and then they're gone. So I go out to our own plants, pick a few, and that's it.

Some of the preserves

"If I could really get organized, I'd figure out for each month of the year or each season what it is that's coming in fresh and then do all the things you want to do because if you only make one thing, you get tired of it. So I make six or eight different things, depending on the size of the crop. One of the things we enjoy is a pasta with eggplant, pine nuts, and cherry tomatoes.

"Eggplant," Ann concluded with a sigh, "is sometimes a 'hard sell,' and it bears pretty heavily, so if you have four or five plants, that's plenty. It tastes good, but to find something to do with it isn't always easy. An Italian friend of ours makes eggplant parmigiana, which I've done occasionally. It's good, but a little heavier and richer than I like."

When writing newspaper articles about gardens, it occurred to me that there are several levels of gardeners, all the way from a person who simply mows a lawn and waters a flower bed to dyed-in-the-wool horticulturists.

The latter category is designated to those who, when asked, "If you had to give up gardening or lose an arm, what would your choice be?"

They routinely answer with a question: "Which arm?"

Ann Morris fits comfortably in that category.

The ornamental-edible landscape at Troll Knoll is here, it's there, it's everywhere. To best see it all without wearing out, one travels in one of the golf cart Piglets.

"The edible garden here is all mixed in with the ornamentals," Ann explained as she takes the wheel of her favorite vehicle, "so if it doesn't look good, it's not going to happen."

And the good-looking requirement extends to ornamental flowers and the handsome four-by-eight-foot waist-high-raised garden bins John made of substantial two-by-six planks nearly twenty years ago.

Planter beds provide

"For lunch yesterday," John smiles, shaking his head, "Ann prepared grilled tuna sandwiches using our lettuce and our peppers, and it was wonderful!"

On the Piglet tour, Ann expounds on the downside of edible gardening. "We've had to deal with creatures—deer, ground squirrels, birds—all kinds of things."

Pointing at some woe-begotten plant specimens, she says, "Those are beans and morning glories that have been chewed down to green spaghetti. So you have to protect them. Initially, we used chicken wire atop the raised beds because one morning I was installing cabbage transplants, and after I returned from my lunch break, they were mowed off at ground level!

"The problem with chicken wire is that it makes it hard for you to get in and plant or harvest. So we switched to polyethylene netting, which is much easier to work with. And to keep it from flapping up in breezy weather, John has attached small lead fishing weights along the bottom.

"But a friend who uses netting to protect her fruit trees found that it became a trap for harmless garden snakes, and she spent a lot of time cutting them loose."

Similarly, during our tour, Ann rescued a sparrow that had become snared in some overly long netting.

Fiery red hot peppers, summer fare which serves more for ornamentation than fare at the Morrises' table, are growing in one raised planter, and tiny kohlrabi transplants are beginning to gain stature at their base.

"As soon as frost comes," Ann explains, "the peppers are gone, and I'll cut off at the base to give the kohlrabi room. The same goes for eggplant, which are removed to make way for brussels sprouts and for tomatoes, with broccoli and cabbages underneath."

This interplanting of seasonal crops is done throughout the garden, with color often supplied by flowers like dianthus and colorful hand-painted wooden sign labels created especially for Troll Knoll by a Southern gardener and artist.

"I love citrus," Ann smiles, "and our grapefruit tree. I'm the only one who drinks it at breakfast. Then we have lemons and oranges tucked in here and there, all over the garden. They're decorative too.

Sometimes reminders help

"We also have sweet cherries, and when they ripen, it's a race with the birds to see who gets them first. So maybe we can try the nets as protection to see how they work. I've been having trouble with birds pulling out tiny transplants in our propagation area, so I used netting but found that when I lifted it, several little slips were uprooted."

Ann brings the Piglet to rest and points to a persimmon tree. "The fruit is *so* hard while it's ripening, but the critters seem to immediately know when it's soft. Maybe, though, we can share the fruit if they just peck at the outside."

There are olive trees in the garden, but they serve a purely ornamental function at present. "I talk to people who have done the curing process, and it seems like a lot of work. When I was growing up on my parents' ranch, there was a row of olive trees, and we used to think it was so funny when Dad coaxed our city friends to taste them!"

Washington navel orange trees, which aren't supposed to grow in Troll Knoll's climate, provide fruit and delicious juice, and they are given no frost protection.

"When it's going to be very cold," Ann offers, "I pick the ripened fruit on the outside branches. We lose some fruit, but it's okay. We have fresh orange juice every single morning from January through April."

Sometimes, though, even Ann's best efforts to grow edibles are thwarted. In the Sunken Garden, for example, summer heat reflecting from the rocky soil was too intense, and it was impossible to keep watered properly with marginal water pressure.

The lemon, orange, and tangerine trees that have survived are now getting more attention than they might have in other parts of the garden.

"When things are planted further away from the house, I like them to be survival-type plants," Ann shares. "If something needs a lot of attention, we may try it once. But if it gives up the ghost, that's it."

Not far away is a plot of ground that was a corn patch. "But we determined very quickly," Ann says with a chuckle, "that corn is very inexpensive at the grocery store. And you have to plant a large amount of it at any one time for it to cross-pollinate. Then it all matures at the same time! So here you've gone to all this work for a few days of harvest."

That area is now dedicated to a waste-recycling pile.

"We throw off a lot of green waste," Ann shrugs, "and so much of it piled up that it attracted snakes. So we brought in a large chipper shredder and either composted it or turned it into mulch for the garden."

The fig orchard produces in marginal soil, and Ann notes, "There are some issues with the birds but not enough to go to the trouble of netting the trees."

On the terrace near the Ruins of Opius VI is a grapevine meant purely for decoration, but Ann says its small grapes are much more flavorful than the large ones from supermarkets.

Nearby is a kumquat tree Ann loves. "That's one of the fun things to do in the garden. Just pick the fruit and snack on it."

The Perennial Garden is dedicated to things like artichokes (harvested in May), along with rhubarb and blueberries (harvested in June).

Troll guarding edibles?

Troll Knoll's orchard contains peaches, pears, apples, and plums. "We started it ten years ago, and it took a while for them to get started because the deer really beat up the trees."

"I wanted to be able to harvest the fruit without getting on ladders," she acknowledges, "so they're pruned to an appropriate height."

Ending the tour and returning her Piglet to the house, Ann smiles, "Today we're going to have a little pizza for lunch, and I'll be going down to the garden to get some fresh ingredients."

Notice something different? Fruits and vegetables are everywhere at Troll Knoll, and there is very little structured vegetables in formal garden areas. For example, Swiss chard is planted as an ornamental and oranges and lemons are planted for color.

A view from the kitchen garden

The street scene by John Holland is almost 16 feet across

To the surprise of some and delight of many, Troll Knoll's "Kitchen Garden" actually begins just a few feet from the kitchen door, offering Ann a handy and delightful assortment of fresh herbs and spices.

Nonetheless, as a favorite spot for dining *al fresco* most of the year, the patio area lacked metaphorical *pizzazz*.

And so it was that John envisioned the stark white wall - which is part of a narrow outdoor utility room - as a *blank canvas*. But what could bring it to life?

The answer came when he was visiting a home and garden show in nearby Auburn and saw the creativity of John Holland, a Lake Tahoe artist who specializes in painting murals.

Creative juices began to flow and it wasn't long before Holland transformed the blank wall into a trompe l'oeil mural depicting a charming street in an old Italian village. And the artwork has been further enhanced by the addition of real potted plants and hanging baskets which expand the scene.

Working for five half-days, with his video camera tracking progress, Holland exceeded the Morris' expectations with his efforts. And, of course, the mural includes some mysterious "Troll Knoll" touches, such as the addition of John and Ann's names and birth years above facing doorways.

"We each come from separate doorways," John says, smiling at the irony, "and meet in the middle of the street."

Another unique feature of the mural is that the white wall had cracked over the years and was slated for repair. Not anymore: The crack serves as a natural border for the mural.

Furthermore, an antique street lamp (identical to one in the mural) has been added to the scene, and a clear Plexiglas cover has been added overhead to protect the mural from the weather.

From there the patio has additional views of the distant Sierra, more tables and umbrellas and numerous other enhancements.

Evening comes to Annsville

Chapter 21

Annsville Honors the Old West

Entrance to Two Dog Mine

As mentioned before, the real purpose of the garden at Troll Knoll was for the owners (whom John often refers to in the third person as Lord and Lady Whackemback) to take evening strolls.

But for a stroll to really have meaning, there must be a destination. It could be as simple as a shaded bench alongside a fountain or something more meaningful, like an entire town from the Old West.

John explains, "What I wanted was to have a retreat from the property to go to. Annsville is one of those areas."

John flashes one of his smiles that come from deep inside and then begins to tell of Annsville's origins when he, during the early stages of retirement, was alone while Ann went to work in Sacramento. Oftentimes she spent weeks in distant cities as chief financial officer for a major medical foundation.

"I was lonely and bored," John recalls, shaking his head. "And I had already done the Ruins of Opius VI. There was no roadway then to where Annsville would be, except for the pathway for concrete trucks to get in and out. One day one of them got stuck, and we had to create a roadway.

"The property was big enough that I wanted a destination on it, so if you started a walk at the house, you'd end up somewhere. It was a backhoe operator who said, 'You oughta do a mine!' I had no idea you could build a mine with a backhoe, but we did. We started in late November, and it took two days to dig the hole. Then along came a fella who had done mining 'sets' for Allegheny. I ordered the timbers he asked for, and without even drawing a line, he took out his chainsaw and went to work. So we finished the timbers and covered the structure with dirt. I intended using it for a wine cellar.

Annsville Sawmill and Taxi Service

"At that point, Ann had never been down there, and she was going to be away on business for six or seven weeks. Our daughter, Stephanie, had outgrown our house here and needed a place of her own to stay on her visits. That led to building the saloon, which started out as a construction building, and then the hotel.

"I stayed down there at nights during the construction and had a carpenter come to help out. I based it on Emerson's *On Golden Pond* and used a little book called *Tiny Houses* (by Lester R. Walker) and sketched out on legal pads what I was going to do. I used my cell phone to order materials, and it went so fast and so well that I was stunned . . . and then was even more stunned when I realized what I had spent, charging it to my American Express card.

"And since Ann is the one who handles the family finances, I knew I would have some explaining to do. It took six weeks to build the structure but two-and-a-half years of planning.

"At that time, you couldn't drive down there, you had to walk. So Ann came home one weekend, and we walked down to look at it. Then I said, 'Ann, there's a Marysville and a Susanville, and I think this should be 'Annsville.' It's a guest house, so you won't have children tearing up your home, and Stephanie can stay there when she comes to visit. Happy Birthday!' And she bought it. She paid the bills and then, if I recall correctly, wasn't down there again for more than a year."

Lobby at the Annsville Hotel

At that time, a ladder served as the entrance to the upstairs bedroom loft, but that has since been replaced by a spiral staircase that John built from a kit. He's a skilled welder, among other things.

Collapse of the Annsville Bank and Trust Co

"By the time Ann returned to Annsville, there was a saloon, district offices, a cemetery, a city park, and the water tower. I'd asked a friend who writes about the Old West if it was missing anything, and she said it needed a schoolhouse. So I built one.

"At that time, I was working on building the trestle for the (authentic) ore cart that served the mine. And every time I'd put in the beams to hold it up, the Rinkydinks (mischievous mythical residents of the knoll) would knock them down within a few days. I told Ann that I was getting tired of this, and it was time to finish the project.

Stairway to Loft

"One of the things I thought would look good there was not to try to make things look brand new but to have them look weathered. And that garden area lent itself to that look very well. So maintenance of Annsville is almost nonexistent."

Another segment of Annsville, the addition of a collapsed Annsville Bank & Trust Co., came about in accord with the financial crisis of 2008. The remnants of the teller's cage, the old empty safe, and other items reflect on that financial episode.

"It was one of the quicker things to build," John shares.

Water tower signals approach to Annsville

"The weather station, donated by Lord and Lady Whackemback, has some clever observations, like being able to detect snow on the ground."

In any case, Annsville does provide a getaway for the couple. "Every once in a while, we spend the night there," John reflects. "It does have a bathroom, kitchen, fireplace, and other accouterments.

"And Annsville fits into the garden's timeline extremely well. If you go down the Old Annsville Road, you pass dinosaur habitats, swamps, Roman ruins, a giant vegetable garden, and then you reach Annsville, which is right before Pinky's Trailer Park and the space station."

And occasionally, the deserted town provides a venue for a special dinner setting.

"Ann plans that we have a meal out in the garden at regular intervals," John explains. "And it's interesting to watch a lady, who is so efficient and well-refined, do that. So over a year's time, there would be sixteen different days we'd go to various areas of the garden to have a meal. Sometimes it would be an elaborate meal, and we'd use the Piglets for transportation. And during the month before arriving, each of the areas would be cleaned up."

The smile on his face is one of fulfillment.

Over by the town cemetery the wagon used to bring occupants to tennis shoe hill

Ore cart crossing

*Wackemback's office
and gold dump
under the trestle*

*Wagon visitor at the
speaker podium*

*Detailing using
Manzanita*

Annsville Station

Annsville fire bell

Johnny's Place

Excalibur

The One Lung Mining Claim and Inside the Ole Two Dog Mine

The graveyard shift works every night, except in late October

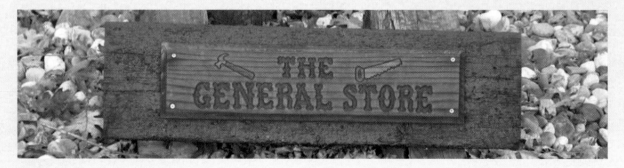

The library in Annsville

Chapter 22

Pinky's Trailer Park

Okay, name another garden that contains a trailer park.

Don't feel bad. I can't either.

Such facilities are common in John's native Mississippi, and he must have been thinking of them in 2001 when, recovering from a series of illnesses, he got on the Internet and decided to "corner the market" on vintage Airstream trailers.

Built like aircraft, Airstreams have a low rounded profile, an aluminum body, and are the crème de la crème of travel trailers. And owners in Delaware, Washington, and Florida who answered John's inquiries were willing to deliver them to Troll Knoll.

"One elderly couple was particularly poignant," John recalls, "because they had been using it for ten years, visiting places on their bucket list, and when they delivered it, a van arrived to take them to the rest home where they would be living. I told them to call if they ever wanted to visit and see it again, but they never have."

As anyone who has ever lived in an old-fashioned trailer park (I did as a child), they all have a telephone booth. John quickly purchased one and has it lit at night. Plus, it plays the *Twilight Zone* theme music on command and has gadgetry on its top like the time-travelling one featured in the sci-fi series *Dr. Who*.

The park is authentic enough that a neighbor spotted it one evening and called the county, alarmed that a *real* trailer park was being established.

"I wish they'd just asked me, instead of going to all that trouble," John says, smiling and shaking his head.

Development continued unabated. Some 250 pink flamingos capture the true trailer park ambiance, as do fences created of old half-buried automobile tires and a pink portable toilet. The neon "Pinky's Trailer Park" sign that John created adds significantly to the décor.

It sounds authentically tacky, but John feels that the landscaping along the Primrose Path will ultimately make Pinky's one of the most photographed parts of the garden.

"Ann is propagating hundreds of Red-Hot Poker plants," John smiles. "They were all the rage in the 1950s. Plus, we'll have oleanders, euryops, rosemary, California poppies, and other plants that are colorful and durable.

"I've been remodeling the interiors of the trailers, and it's much more difficult than I imagined because of the precise way they're built."

Plans were to have one serve as a mini-movie theater where the Morrises would enjoy watching DVDs, but it proved to be too confining. It's now being used as guest quarters. One was going to be a beer parlor, but Ann's sensibilities prevailed, and now it's Ann's Wine and Spirits Bar.

"The third," John says, eyes twinkling, "is our space station. That's where the hot tub is, to keep our extraterrestrial visitors comfortable."

Ann's Wine and Spirits Bar

Every luxury cruise ship has a cozy getaway for intimate gatherings. Fine wines, soft music, and romantic lighting create an atmosphere for relaxation.

Such is the case for the good ship Troll Knoll, where a remodeled Airstream trailer in Pinky's Trailer Park fills that need. Originally slated to be a Troll beer hall (an idea squelched by Lady Whackemback), the venue, now known as Ann's Wine and Spirits Bar, offers the latest wi-fi hookup, an electronic dartboard, heating and air-conditioning, and a fascinating musical playlist emanating from various speakers.

Originally, the 1984 Airstream was dubbed simply as Ann's Wine Bar, but although the owners are particularly keen on the pleasures afforded by Kendall-Jackson Chardonnay wine, among others, they've also taken a liking to a pricey Belgian pale ale marketed under the appropriate name of Cuvee des Trolls.

One beer connoisseur describes it this way: "The bubbles are rather sedate, the body a decent medium weight, and generally pretty smooth. It finishes off dry, the bready pale malt still most prevalent, as the yeast and hops dwindle to a dull echo."

An intimate lounge, which seats four comfortably, fills what was the trailer's bedroom and also offers the comfort of a small fireplace. There are fluffy cushions on padded benches that have been modified to allow a person of Lady Whackemback's diminutive stature to sit with feet firmly on the floor.

And like the Old Annsville Hotel and other structures, it's equipped with an ultrasonic rodent-deterring device.

Does it work?

"We'll see," John offers.

The old hi-fidelity speakers have been removed from the trailer in favor of the latest electronics. "I can plug into the Internet," John explains, "and go to Pandora's for crisp, clean music without the hum of the old speakers. I have a Logitech device that works all the speakers. It's kinda cool!"

While this book was in the making, it was obvious that John had overcome what he describes as a two-year mental block concerning the development of the bar and of Pinky's Trailer Park. The area is freshly graveled, and just around the corner sat a twenty-yard mountain of potting soil meant to "get things growing."

Coolaroos float twenty-feet high above the trailers, prepared for summer. Developed in Australia, the triangular pieces of colorful fabric are moved into place by a network of ropes and pulleys to afford the trailers the most amount of shade, thus cutting air-conditioning costs.

"I got thirty of them through Overstock.com," John explains with a satisfied grin. "And to enhance the night garden, they'll be lit from underneath. We have to be concerned about the wind coming up and doing damage, so I also want it so they can be taken down."

Outside the trailer, a rocky embankment is slated to be festooned with succulents. Right across Old Annsville Road is the polka-dot lawn growing within metal barrel staves, just above the bottle garden area.

John notes that every one of the many vignettes within the garden is hinged to some aspect of his life, and this fanciful creation using hundreds of empty wine bottles reflects the "days of wine and roses" when bubbly flowed more frequently at Troll Knoll than now.

The bottles will add to the mystery of the night garden, illuminated by strings of LED lights. The host of plastic pink flamingos a few yards away will get the same treatment.

Pinky's telephone booth will also be illuminated, further enhanced with a revolving antenna on its top, beamed at the trailers to do its thing.

Horticulturally, the area will be emblazoned by the addition of summer bloomers, including oleanders, agapanthus, and red-hot pokers.

"When everything's in place," John says in satisfaction, "I suspect this will be the most photographed area of the entire garden!"

Cranking up the Wine Bar

Time in a Bottle

A large white plastic bag caught my eye one morning as I pulled into Troll Knoll's driveway. It was full of empty wine bottles.

John was emerging from the house to greet me and saw the puzzled look on my face.

"Those are from our neighbors," he explained with a laugh, "who learned we're building a bottle garden at Pinky's Trailer Park."

And among the multitude of attractions at Pinky's, the bottle garden provokes a lot of comments from visitors.

The only other time I'd seen a bottle garden before this was on the web page of my friend Felder Rushing (www.felderrushing.net), a Mississippi gardener who, like me, has achieved fellow status with the prestigious Garden Writers Association. In fact, he's written a book on the subject, *Bottle Trees and Other Whimsical Glass Art for the Garden*.

His research shows that glass was manufactured as early as 3500 BC in Northern Africa, and bottles appeared around 1600 BC in Egypt and Mesopotamia. Clear glass didn't show up until around AD 100 in Alexandria.

The mournful sounds made when wind blew across the open mouths of bottles inspired the thought that genies and such could be captured in them while they roamed by night. As the tale begs us to believe, they couldn't escape and would ultimately be eliminated by the morning's light.

This story was reportedly spread through sub-Saharan Africa and was brought to our shores by African slaves.

To some, they're simply bottles on sticks. To others, there are deeper meanings.

In any case, the Morrises were shocked to find that sunlight focused by the glass was hot enough to start fires in adjacent foliage. A liberal use of gravel beneath them has lessened that hazard.

Exactly how the bottle garden is being received by the Far Western Rinkydinks who live not far away has yet to be determined.

Pinky's under construction

The flamingos roam freely through the meadows

Preparing for the visitors

the new neon sign and tire fencing in place

The Mother Ship

Chapter 23

Troll Knoll's X-Files

To those familiar with the timeline of Troll Knoll, the UFO Garden seems to be a likely conclusion of a trip that starts with dinosaurs at one end and winds up—past Annsville and Pinky's Trailer Park—with visitors from outer space.

Not so. What we have is a sort of Mobius strip time loop in which the end is really the beginning.

"The saucers were here before the dinosaurs," John tells visitors of the disc-shaped spaceships.

And then he explains how the craft came into being. First, although admittedly investing "a handsome hunk of change" into the garden, John is frugal at heart. (Ann's dismay is he hates to throw things away.)

"When I took down the old disc-shaped satellite antennas for the television," he says with a wave of his hands, "I realized that when you put two of them together, you have what looks like a flying saucer. Then I briefly advertised on radio that I wanted old satellite dishes and got more than I could use. But before I was able to start construction, one of them got crushed in the moving process. So that one's embedded in the ground, as if it had crashed. And you see the mother ship and two smaller ones involved in a rescue mission."

A friend at Lake's Nursery had donated some old steel pipe to the garden, and that was used for legs to suspend the mother ship fourteen feet above the ground. And John had scored a deal buying some collapsible ladders to use as folding legs for the smaller craft, from which some transponder robots donning straw hats and tennis shoes are apparently walking to the crash scene.

And not far off is a towering white missile, largely created with cast-off water pump equipment and other materials.

"We constantly have water pumps giving up the ghost." John sighs. "So the reservoirs are painted white and welded with stainless steel tubs alongside as motors.

"We have a lot of Christmas tree lights we no longer need since our home is largely decorated for Christmas all year," John says, drawing a deep breath. "And they're used out here on the flying saucers and the missile. They're hooked up to motion sensors, so when deer and other animals pass through, they come on and blink for forty-five seconds. I imagine people driving along Highway 20 at night are often surprised by what appears to be a missile popping up out of the ground."

And is this the last major addition to the garden?

"I don't walk to the beat of anyone else's drum," John says, his eyes crinkling at the corners. "A project like the pond for Pinky's Trailer Park was started thirteen years ago, and we're just starting to fill it with water now. Who cares? But it is time to be done, so I'll be operative at that level forthwith."

Interpret that as a big "Maybe."

Ship Too with its Straw hatted and tennis shoe Transponders

They search day and night thru all weather

Largely recognized for mischievous borrowing of garden tools, or undoing tasks that have been done, the Far Western Rinkydinks are peaceful creatures who simply want to be left alone. To protect themselves from dinosaurs, for example, they hired friendly dragons.

170

Chapter 24

The Far Western Rinkydinks

In the early days of our friendship, I recall John making mention of the Rinkydinks in reference to some plan that had gone awry. And this band of mischief-makers has been cited for various misdeeds over the ensuing years, up to and including walking off with a string trimmer.

Who are they? What are they up to? Most importantly, why do they feel so inclined to scamper off with some of the Troll's most precious tools?

"When we first moved to Troll Knoll and moved into the House of No Gremlins, it should have been clear that all was not as you might imagine," John explains, "or maybe it was. You would try to find a tool, and it would not be where you expected it to be. You would take someone to show them the interesting formation, and it would appear to be gone. You would trip on a rock that you did not know was there.

"In my particular experience, I would build a small structural item, and it would be in pieces when it was next seen. Electrical items were of particular concern. This went on for a very long time.

A guard dragon protects the Village of Far Western Rinkydinks

"One day on a walk through the manzanita looking for paths, there was a beautiful specimen of a woodpecker drilling on an old burned pine tree. He looked at me, I looked at him, and then I tripped on a rock. The woodpecker did not quit drilling. I got up and went around to get a better look. I tripped again. The woodpecker quit drilling and looked at me. As I got up, the woodpecker moved around to the other side of that tree and looked around as if to say, 'Leave me alone or they will do it again.'

"As I slid down for the third time, it was obvious that there was something different about the area. Little did I know that I was in the area known as the Lands of the Far Western Rinkydinks, a tribe without comparison.

"During the excavation of the village of the Far Western Rinkydinks, I found the reason the tribe and its elders located where they did. Recalling the words of the elders led by Professor Nosebeter and the chants that move, there are many, many references to the area.

"Marked with a petrified tree stone with the village surrounding it is the Center of the Known Universe," John explains. "With the chaos swirling around, the Rinkydinks feel grounded and safe, for they are at the center. Everything revolves around the village, also known as the Homeland. I feel privileged to live so close to the Homeland and CKU (Center of the Known Universe)."

Notable among the village residents are the Whimseys, Pearl and Fred, along with Flora and Fauna Smythe, happily married women whose garden is the envy of the neighborhood, and Blythe and Thomas Outcast, whose home sits apart from the others.

There's a saying, "If you can't whip 'em, join 'em!" and John is, thus, adding another vignette to the garden, close to the Rocket Garden, building homes for the unseen residents.

"Maybe they would look something like the Troll houses you see elsewhere," John says. "I'm thinking of ways to make smoke come out of the chimneys . . ."

Troll Knoll's Nature Trail

Another bastion of defense created by the Far Western Rinkydinks long, long ago is a formidable poison oak grove along the Troll Knoll Nature Walk. That's why the path circling the perimeter of the domain is seldom trod by casual visitors. Another reason, since it's best accessed near the UFO Garden where tours traditionally end, is that guests are both physically and mentally fatigued. Finally, it's up- and downhill and challenging enough to be a good tune-up for the famed Tevis Run, in which one hundred miles of rugged countryside are covered—on foot—in one day. Except to supervise maintenance of the trail, the Troll seldom traverses its length from beginning to end.

"Its true purpose," he explains, "is to allow fire equipment to get into difficult areas without having to cut through underbrush with a fire in progress."

About the poison oak meadow, Lord Whackemback adds, "Lady Whackemback is paying close attention that I use whatever means possible to eliminate it."

Other than that, nature's craftsmanship will be augmented at strategic locations by wildflowers (from seed purchased by the pound) and the Troll's buttermilk and Miracle-Gro treatment on some handsome boulders to inspire a mossy demeanor.

Beware the Knolls

"The village of the Far Western Rinkydinks is important for several reasons," John explains, "primarily that it's located at the Center of the Known Universe.

"They landed there long ago, set up their village, and were living quietly until the Troll decided to move in up on the hill."

Another dragon protecting the Knolls

Backing the narrative up a bit, John supplies some history: "There was a migration of Trolls from the eastern coast. And during the original battle for Troll Knoll, the Wonderful Witch of the West turned them all into stone, and they're still there, locked into the stone."

Speaking from experience, he adds, "If you kick one, it'll hurt you!"

Further complicating things, the Troll brought in some dinosaurs, known enemies of Rinkydinks, who sought protection by employing friendly dragons. Still, the dragons were outnumbered, and it was rumored that humans were joining the invasion. And everyone knows how Rinkydinks regard humans, thus began an ebb and flow of all manner of creatures, including some disguised as shrubs.

"The leader of the Far Western Rinkydinks thought if they could frighten the humans away, maybe they'd take the dinosaurs with them," John explains, adding, "the thought was if they all mooned the humans, they'd depart. Or they could transform the backsides of their houses into big creatures called Knolls.

"Further bolstering their defenses, they created human traps using irresistible giant M&Ms as a lure, with a trip hammer device to clobber unsuspecting people. And any humans who were captured would be put into a Rinkydink hot seat (which closely resembles a ratty office swivel chair with a small BBQ on the seat).

"And that," John concludes with a broad smile, "is a prime example of a conceptual metaphor!"

They're everywhere at Troll Knoll. Children can spot them faster than most adults.

The Human Trap

What do the statue and the missle have in common?

Chapter 25

The Night Garden

The Morrises' extensive collection of garden books has several that discuss the Night Garden but disappointingly so.

"They mostly talk about planting a variety of white-flowered plants that can be seen by moonlight," John sighs, "and it's usually for a small garden room area."

That's not what the Morrises have in mind for Troll Knoll. For their romantic evening walks, they want to enjoy the plants and the hardscape and to see where they're going.

And no, simply putting some traditional garden lamps along the pathways won't do the trick.

Much of this information was gathered while John, who did virtually all the wiring at Troll Knoll, was standing atop a tall extension ladder wearing a bulky white multipurpose vest overflowing with wires, switches, lightbulbs, and tools. He was replacing a burned-out light.

"We have 260 garden lights on the property," he estimates, "and at one time, if we turned everything on, the electricity cost about $35 a night."

Now using various types of lights and timers, it costs a fraction of that.

"The night garden is like the others," John continues, "except its purpose is to allow us to enjoy the garden after dark. It's strange that we have over an hour more summer daylight here than we did in Mississippi, but the reverse is true in winter."

When the power and electrical grid was laid out for Troll Knoll, it provided electrical outlets every eighty feet, so all manner of lighting possibilities exist: colorful lights on statuary, such as *Kwan Yin*; lights for the pathways; lights to show angels playing musical instruments; and security lights to ward off uninvited visitors, like hungry deer nibbling vegetables and ornamentals. And for his neighbors' sake, John has refrained from using dramatic red and yellow spotlights in the Dinosaur Habitat.

Some—like the marine lights at Pond Won, originally purchased for a wharf in Mississippi—are quite expensive. The same can be said for LED lighting and halogen lamps, but John feels they've made incandescent lighting obsolete.

"The new eco-bulbs can replace a 40-watt light with one that uses 7.5 watts," he says.

And the lighting scheme is purposefully designed to blend with lights from communities, twinkling in the distance.

Evening pastels blend and then become night

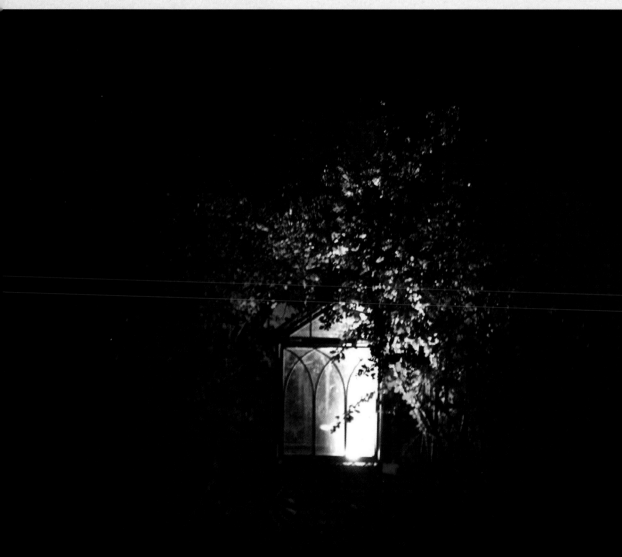

On the evening walks, there are many lighting effects.

The Ruins of Opius VI makes a evening destination

The atrium colonnade in early evening

There was way too much effort put out and spent on this garden to only see it during the day.

Many lighting effects are used

190

Chapter 26

Is It Worth a Wooden Nickel?

Almost every realm has its own coinage. And that's true of Troll Knoll.

John has designed and coined his own wooden nickels, thousands of them.

The coins are imprinted with "Troll Knoll Garden Pass" on one side and display the patriotic words "*E. Pluribus Unum*" (From many, one.).

The other side pictures the profile of an American buffalo. Also included is the www.trollknoll.com website (a tribute to modern technology) together with a salute to John Muir, the Yosemite Valley, and the words, "Official Annsville Currency."

That's a salute to the historic Old West community he built as a surprise birthday present for Ann.

What is their purpose? John explains, "When I was growing up, my parents always offered the advice, 'Don't take any wooden nickels!' that grew out of the great depression when banks gave them to customers to lure them back and eventually cash in for premiums.

"Because of the whimsy in me, I had them coined as tokens to hand out to garden visitors who ask a particularly good question or make a suggestion about how to improve the garden. They are a garden pass for return visitors and my way of saying, 'Be safe, be careful, and have a good journey.'"

Chapter 27

Preparing for the Prom

We met in John's office in February, and he was discussing how he had turned down several recent requests to visit the garden.

"I told them, 'I'm getting ready for the prom,'" he says, laughing. "In essence, we have two daughters—our Stephanie and Troll Knoll."

And there are remarkable similarities in preparing a young woman for presentation at an event like a prom or debutante ball or getting a garden ready for viewing at its peak of season.

"What you see in February," he explains, "is the garden like a young woman getting a bath (from rainfall) and putting on ribbons (flowers) getting ready for the big date.

"Yesterday I spent several hours getting the proper combs, hair curlers, and dress for the garden," he continues with a smile, "and this afternoon, I'll get Eddie (the tractor) and dress the roads with gravel road base."

Actually, there are some twenty tons of road base waiting to be distributed around the garden, and next to the garage is an assortment of tuned-up garden power tools fresh from the local saw shop.

"I've got weed eaters, trimmers, blowers . . . all ready to go," he says with a satisfied grin, "and I've done this for so many years that I really don't want help. And the result will be like people seeing the beautiful young girl at the prom. But they won't see the nuances that go into the planning for the big event.

"What I'll be doing to the garden now is like Ann and I helping our daughter with her hair, adding bows and ribbons and flowers for the big event. That's what goes on for the next two months in the garden, like scattering wildflower seed (one hundred pounds of it) in strategic locations.

"Because of time limitations, we'll have fewer tours than any time over the past ten years. We've got things to do like styling rose trellises at the Three Graces. Ann is hard at work on the fruit orchard, and I'm eager to put our new electric jackhammer to work—if I'm able to handle it."

Drawing a breath, he continues, "People sometimes confuse Troll Knoll with a public garden. It's not. It's a real garden . . . a home garden that's being presented for viewing. And at times, when it's not ready, people can go to our website at www.trollknoll.com and get a preview."

What can we say? The visits make the garden fun.

By the time folks reach Annsville, they have walked two hours and well over a mile

The attire depends on the age of the group visiting

Socializing and leading groups make a Troll happy

A California Postcard production. Note the boxers are part of the production.

and more and more

A jumbled old rock wall on the high heel walk

Chapter 28

The Topic Is Neatness

A Monterey gardener I once interviewed had a garden designed by famed landscape architect Thomas Church.

Unlike traditional Church gardens that rely mostly on the colors gray and green, this one had pockets of floral color created by the owner.

Despite the fact Church's own garden had more color than those he designed for clients, seeing flowers in his gardens unsettled some purists.

"One day I was working in the garden and heard someone coming through the gate," the owner grimaced, "and I wasn't expecting guests. But a well-dressed woman was standing in the gateway with her eyes sweeping the scene. I asked if I could help her, but she didn't answer. She just said, 'Well! I've never seen such a *mess* in my life!'

"I then told her she hadn't been invited to my garden and to go away."

Some visitors at Troll Knoll react in similar fashion when they find a pile of clippings on a pathway or stumble upon an equipment service area. They're unconsciously measuring a private garden with the same yardstick one might use at Filoli, Chanticleer, Giverny, or Butchart Gardens.

Those gardens have work crews. Troll Knoll has only Lord and Lady Whackemback.

John shakes his head when he recalls one such incident: "A fellow who harvests our grapes to make wine came over to check out the vineyard. When we walked up the driveway to see the new outdoor kitchen in the patio garden, he asked why we hadn't built a cover so the table would be out of the sun, and I pointed out the umbrellas we use in June and July. And I showed him other shaded eating places we have, like the Four Seasons patios, the Three Graces, the Boulder Cafe in Provence, and a rooftop-covered patio we call the veranda.

*Balustrade overlooks surround
the walks in key views*

203

The salmon run in the Stream of Words

Good fairies stop the leaks

Stacks of calla lilies and water irises by the frog dance floor

Some pigs need to hold on

207

They get the idea

Beach front property at the bridge of streaming faces

No vineyard, fiber optics, asphalt paths and such' for the heavy equipment picture.

Chapter 29

Inside the Knoll's "Engine Room"

"Of the hundreds of gardens you've visited," John said during one of our Wednesday morning meetings, "I'll wager this is the first one in which you've seen the inner workings in all seasons, in all states of preparedness."

He's right.

Picture Troll Knoll as a giant luxury cruise liner with a mission of keeping passengers safe, comfortable, wined, dined, and entertained—who, for the most part, are completely unaware of all the work that goes on below decks.

The good ship Troll Knoll doesn't have the huge crew of a luxury liner, only the efforts of Lord and Lady Whackemback and on-again-off-again part-time help for heavy labor keep the vessel moving.

"Let me show you what I've been doing," John says, unrolling an overlay that is a bewildering blueprint detailing the Knoll's plumbing and electrical layout.

"This plan came about because when we planned the garden, I had all the lines, including propane for the house, all laid out. Then we added soil at the house site to allow us to build a one-story home."

Eyebrows raising, he draws a sigh. "Which meant that some lines are as much as forty-feet deep. So it's easy to lose track of things, like a controller which I recalled was by the front of a pond. After three years of searching, we hired an electrician to trace the wiring and found it fifteen feet from where we thought it was, covered in a foot of soil."

And the reason it was covered was John's habit of blowing deeply when using a backpack leaf blower to clean the pathways. That means blowing the debris off the path, then giving it another blast so it becomes compost for the plants. It's a technique he picked up watching Ann's mother care for her garden.

"It adds neatness and refinement when the paths have sharp edges," he explains.

There are also problems like coping with rodents that were apt to make meals of wiring within the garden's several shelters. There had been sonic devices installed in each one that are supposed to keep them at bay.

"I'll believe it when I see it" is John's assessment. "When you have a cruise ship, you have to plan for maintenance."

Your mother isn't here. Please clean up and carry away your own messes

*The General Store...that is
not a general*

The Chemical Cottage,
inside and out

Chapter 30

Troll Knoll Snapshots

Eddie, the tractor

With trolls, being the imaginative creatures they are, there's no end to the examples of whimsy one might find, or totally overlook, on a tour of the garden.

And that's how it was planned.

"The only straight path here is the entrance to the atrium," John says. "Everything else is curved, so visitors have to look at the paths and ponds. My perspective is you don't want to see the whole collection at once. In addition to being a sanctuary, a garden is a collection of things like statuary and the Wardian cases."

Along Old Annsville Road, for example, is a sign for the What Garden, which is a number of ornate wooden question marks sitting atop steel pegs. This is nothing more than the Troll acknowledging he has a hearing problem and is constantly asking Ann "What?"

Garden fairies are another of the somewhat elusive (it's their nature, you see) residents on the knoll.

"These ladies of Troll Knoll are miniatures in bronze and other materials that are scattered throughout the garden," John says, smiling. "I don't want to come across them every day. They're entertainment and a comfort food for me, like macaroni and cheese."

The Arboretum too might be overlooked for most of the year. In fact, it was somewhat of a disappointment for John for ten years, but now its color display for a month or so in autumn rivals the impact of springtime in other areas.

The tools of the trade really aren't really garden attractions, but without the implements, like the Rollinator (used for moving large pots and boulders), the Piglets, and Eddie the Tractor, the workload might have been insurmountable.

(About Eddie, John recalls using it to work on the Tennis Shoe Walk, originally the perimeter pathway, when it went freewheeling on an unexpected visit downhill to Highway 20. "After that, I stopped working on the walk. I was terrified!"

Streaming faces

Although intended largely for maintenance, the Tennis Shoe Walk is dotted with citrus trees and roses, making for a colorful diversion on summer walks.

The Pump House usually rates merely a glance from garden visitors but deserves more attention. "It's only ten by ten feet," John says, shaking his head, "but is more costly per square foot than any other building on the property. It's linked to the solar panels, the pump system, and the electrical network for that part of the property. To replace it would cost about $250,000."

Flags and umbrellas spice up the garden's color scheme. The flags are zinnias, one of the few uses of annuals in the garden, and fourteen umbrellas are used for shade at the Three Graces fountain, the Kitchen Garden, and at Provence.

"We replace two or three of them every year because of wind and sun damage," John says with a shrug.

Carriages and wagons located in Annsville came from Montana, where John was on a fishing trip and spotted a collection being sold by its elderly owner.

"They add to the ambiance of the old mining town," John acknowledged, "and I like to do woodworking, so I plan to restore them."

Daffodil Park was planted with a power auger one afternoon, and now there are thousands of them creating a colorful carpet under oaks in springtime.

"Even more beautiful is the fact that they need no irrigation," John says, grinning.

Bus stops, Piglets and boxers—the three Piglets, as you've already learned, are electric golf carts for transportation and drayage throughout the garden. They have routine bus stops for offloading materials, which Pepper and Plato (the Troll's boxers) frequently sit at while awaiting rides back uphill to the house.

Patios are an important part of the landscape scheme. "There's one for every day of the week," John explained, "and being circular allows one to head out in different directions. They cause a creative poke in the tummy over what to do with the other stuff in the area."

Balustrades and overlooks were imported in parts from Silvestri's and installed at points with the most commanding views of the garden, the valley and far-off mountain ranges like the Siskiyous, the Sierra Nevada, and the Sutter Buttes.

In addition to all these things are features that died on the drawing board.

"I had an idea about routing a stream through the house," John says, chuckling, "but the estimates for its construction were higher than the cost of the house.

Two brothers cafe

"And because of the wonderful view of the Milky Way from here, I really pondered over building a small observatory."

The look in his eye and sound of his voice gave the impression that the idea may someday gain new life.

"Troll Knoll Dragons came into being," John explains, "is when numerous visitors called the dinosaurs dragons."

Then he found the original metal dragon at a nursery and installed her between the dinosaurs and the Far Western Rinkydinks. It's obvious she's a female since she has eggs, which only a few astute visitors recognize.

It seemed logical to John that the female would need a male companion, but he was unable to find one.

"So I had him fabricated in Southern Mexico," John shares. "You can tell he's a male because he has wings to fly around with."

The Far Western Rinkydinks, meanwhile, were edgy about the dinosaurs and cut a deal with the dragons to protect them. Since that time, plans were laid to install a hybrid two-headed dragon-dinosaur in a nearby tree. How the addition of a third fire-breathing creature will affect the current pact is as yet unknown.

Provence has a story as romantic as its name: "Once upon a time, I wanted to live in Provence," John explains. "Ann and I had visited France and enjoyed Paris but really fell in love with the region around Aix en Provence. In fact, I'd signed a ninety-nine-year-lease on a lovely farm there, but then there was an emotional tug-of-war whether to live there or here at Troll Knoll."

The lease on the farm was vacated, and the focus shifted to Troll Knoll.

However, a patio with a view that reminds them of outdoor dining at the Two Brothers Cafe in Aix en Provence pays tribute to what might have been.

Two large boulders on the patio represent the Two Brothers, "Where Ann and I thoroughly enjoyed ourselves," John concludes.

Troll Knoll International Raceway—equipped with staging lights and digital timers, the nearly two-mile course on garden paths was launched for a genuine racer from China that proved to be far too fast for the circuit.

Now it's a garden tractor raceway. Roaring around at between five and six miles per hour, the vehicles zip through the Lombardi Curve, down to Annsville, and over to the Oak Tree Turnaround, providing fun for children of all ages.

Troll Knoll Express is the name of an assortment of garden carts towed behind a garden tractor. Its load will include such things as debris headed for the burn pile, building materials, artifacts needing movement, trash cans, all manner of plants, and small grandchildren (whose mother throws her hands up in despair at their adventures with grandpa.)

Tour groups never see it in action because the engineer is leading them through the garden.

The Human Trap is easily seen from Annsville Road, just before entering the western town. Its bait: irresistible colorful giant-sized M&M candies scattered on the ground.

Knowing that humans can't resist the treats that "melt in your mouth, not in your hand," the Far Western Rinkydinks, who live just a few feet away from the Center of the Known Universe, have erected a hammer device to disable anyone who ventures near.

Visitors are advised to beware.

Just another wagon in the woods

In the Southern Arboreum

When you leave Provence, you go
across the bridge to the Western
Gardens at Troll Knoll and encounter
the Streaming Faces. It is one of
many conceptual metaphors.

Chapter 31
Troll Knoll's Hidden Treasures

When guests are being taken on a tour of Troll Knoll, they're usually like kids opening Christmas presents one after another: "Great! What's next?"

And in the excitement, a lot of the whimsy that delights John and Ann is overlooked.

I offer this from experience. Few people have visited the garden more than I, yet on each trip, something new captures my attention, and John nods with a grin when I ask, "Has that been here all along?"

On the far side of the Swamp Garden, for example, is a froggie troubadour happily strumming a mandolin—one of my favorites. But it wasn't until John pointed them out that I saw there's an entire amphibian quartet of musicians silently serenading passersby.

"I'm thinking of a way I can set up a CD to play Mexican music as we pass by," John said, chuckling.

The same goes for ponds. When John mentioned there were eight ponds on the property, I was at a loss locating them. There's Pond Won, of course, along with the Boxer Bog and the Swamp Garden. But where were the others? John explained they're largely overlooked because of being near the less-visited Troll Knoll International Raceway and Dinosaur Garden, and several were so full of cattails and aquatic plants, normally removed in spring, that the water was barely visible.

Ponds number four through seven are stair-stepped down the hillside, connected by hidden pipes. Ultimately, they will be joined by vernal pools if all goes according to plan. Plans do go awry at times, such as the effort to establish water lotus in pond number four. At seven feet, it's the deepest of all, but the lotus didn't take a liking to the location.

Pond number seven boasts of having an enormous rock slab, probably forty feet across, which is fed by a natural winter stream. In non-drought years, water spills over the slab.

And pond number eight, adjacent to the telephone booth in Pinky's Trailer Park, has yet to be filled. And because of the drought, it may remain a pond in name only for the immediate future. However, in typical Troll fashion, rumors are in the air that hundreds of rubber ducks may float on Pond Eight.

"We created the ponds when we were digging soil to create a pad for the house," John expounded. "And it took some investigation to find spots that had a good clay base to hold water and no rock outcroppings."

As we completed our Piglet tour of the ponds, John pulled to a halt and gazed around. "The self-satisfaction of having worked on this so hard and for so long is that now it's everything I wanted it to be."

Visitors play day and night

Below the vineyard

One of several occupants of Lizard Lake

Above--without Ann's oversight (the gardener's shadow)...' and
'below-many days provide this rainbow view

From its's head waters the flow of the Stream of Words provides its annual Salmon Run vista

Without the folks coming to visit and enjoy the garden, there would be no hidden treasures to be found.

Fairies, witches and things abound

Chapter 32

Things We Need to Say

"Chances are . . ." is an often-used phrase. It is important to consider this as a lifestyle rather than a garden, and one is forewarned that it is not a garden for the faint of heart. The dedication of energy is not for everyone, but you might want to consider its benefits. The substantial health benefits and social contacts are worthwhile to the occupants here.

Do you recall Pond Three, the Swamp Garden and Boxer Bog? Chapters 18 and 17? In 2003, this is the look.

Why Knolls Are Here

An Explanation by Lord Wackemback

In the time before Oz and when the orbs had risen in the quest of the universe and there was a consistent pulse in the strings of the spatial integrity in the relevant factors, the extenders of the carbon-based chains revealed the Rinkydinks. It was a time of great consistency. It was a time when the village only needed the protection of the dragons and the Tribe. The influences flowed and ebbed to the orbs, and the rules remained constant. Certainly, it was before the humans passed through the gates and brought havoc, chaos, and the theories of confusion and disbelief so close to the Center of the Known Universe. The Rinkydinks were in disbelief that such an event would be allowed so close to the Center of the Known Universe. Hordes of humans overran the planet and threatened the disruption of the theories of Professor Nosebeter, much like the Martians had done so many eons before. The vibrations turned trees to stone, began to heat the planet, and began to vibrate the strings of the spatial integrity throughout the universe.

What were the Rinkydinks to do? More dragons? Who would feed them? Where would they sleep? Could they overcome the dinosaurs and lizards?

The Elders met and conferred. The tribe, a very hardy tribe of Far Western Rinkydinks, would consolidate The Village, banding together and having the backside of the homes appear as Knolls, the vicious protectors of Rinkydinks and known human-eaters. They would be known as the Group of Seventeen and dedicated to be defenders of The Village, blasting meteors at dinosaurs and lizards. The Elders further established a cunning trap of fake M&Ms to bonk the humans attempting to enter the Lands of the Far Western Rinkydinks and approach the wondrous Village. It was decided that the humans would suffer the Hot Seat and be bound to serve in the Center for Conceptual Metaphors until there were no more. To those ends, all was done, and the universe would soon stable again. The Elders are all-knowing and wise. To be at the Center of the Known Universe most certainly has its advantages. It is forever.

About Troll Knoll's Garden Writer

A note from John Morris

Why do you need a loving wife, a garden writer, paths, boxers, Piglets, vignettes, five tractors, seven hedge clippers, Rinkydinks, and dinosaurs? It takes a mix of ingredients to cook into a garden like Troll Knoll.

Troll Knoll has many unique items of interest. One of those is its own personal garden writer. It did not start that way. Once, he picked on the Troll because of the cereal bowl left from a Troll's breakfast in the tree limbs. We are honored to say that the garden writer has adopted us as gardeners. Dick Tracy has written about Troll Knoll without thought of compensation or personal benefit other than sharing his experience. Of course, he has written about many gardens over the years and has experienced many, many vistas and views of gardens. For several years, he has been a foremost advocate of what this garden is. Ann and I are grateful beyond words for his humor, insight, and company. This book would not be if it did not have the Garden Writer and his recorder to document our sanctuary, hoping to inspire others to do their place on this earth.

Years in the making, encouragement to "let people see" our garden, and concepts while promoting by his articles, our garden has made a huge impact on what we have done. The story and explanation by the Garden Writer of our garden is wonderful and as important as boxers, Piglets, and garden paths. Who needs ladders, hedge clippers, and other such tools when you have a Dick Tracy?

By: Nancy Degenkolb

Chapter 33

"Dick Tracy? Are you kidding?"

Yes, that's my name. And I was named after my father, not a chisel-chinned comic strip police detective.

Now here's how I got to Troll Knoll.

Fate, not gardening expertise, threw me into the role of garden writer for the *Sacramento Bee* newspaper in 1969. And as luck would have it, I thoroughly enjoyed a thirty-year career in that role.

I'd taken a semester of botany at school, but none of that information had really taken root (pun absolutely intended). And everything I knew about gardens could be summed up in a single compound sentence.

At first, a little disheartened by the assignment, I quickly learned that gardeners are wonderful, sharing people.

And over the years, I enjoyed visits to gardens of all sizes in California and other parts of the country. Plus, my "celebrity" cast me in the role of cohost for garden tours in England, Scotland, Wales, France, Italy, New Zealand, and in this country.

When the University of California launched its Master Gardener program in Sacramento, I enrolled and ultimately became a Lifetime Honorary UC Master Gardener.

Joining the Garden Writer's Association, I was elected to direct activities of the Western states and was ultimately named a fellow of the organization. After interviewing Napa Valley luminary Molly Chappellet about her first book, she invited me to join in writing the award-winning *Gardens of the Wine Country*.

Upon retirement, I did some freelance writing for various publications and, in 2004, paid my first visit to Troll Knoll, meeting John and Ann Morris.

They'd graciously opened their garden to support the local Soroptimists' fund-raiser that benefits young women headed to college.

As I walked the grounds with John and realized the size and imagination of the garden, I urged that it be opened more frequently than once a year.

The Morrises agreed, and more than fifty thousand visitors have delighted in free tours led by the Troll.

At one point, I noted I'd never seen a garden like it in all my travels and said, "You ought to write a book about Troll Knoll."

Drawing a deep breath while nodding in agreement, he said, "I love to talk . . . but I hate to type."

"John, I can type," was my response.

That led to Wednesday morning meetings, in which John would focus on various areas of the garden, with our conversation captured by my tape recorder.

Then I'd head for home and start writing.

This system worked beautifully, except on one occasion when John unexpectedly launched into explaining what it meant for him to be out working in the garden. It was sheer poetry.

I glanced down at the recorder, making sure it was running, and then hurried home to put it on paper. To my horror, the recorder's batteries were weak. They supplied enough power to make the tape advance, but it was blank.

The happy thing is that John shares those sentiments with every tour group that walks the pathways at Troll Knoll.

Do you see what being at Troll Knoll does to you?

Dino the belligerent dinosaur

(A Troll Knoll fable)

Dino lives in a magical place called Troll Knoll. It's a little kingdom where a Troll records the activities of a tribe of Far Western Rinkydinks, dragons, gremlins, Knolls and dinosaurs.

Dino has grown up under the care of his uncle Sinclair in the absence of his parents (whom he doesn't know are now extinct) and was well cared for. Except, his uncle Sinclair has never taught him manners.

If he was in the Rinkydink village, he'd roar a fearsome roar and swish his powerful green tail, knocking things- including Rinkydinks – over. Thus, he had an image problem. And the Rinkydink children would laugh and call him names, and goad the dragons into knocking HIM over on occasion.

Dino had no one to play with and wasn't very happy very often.

But one day, as he was sniffing about the crash site of a UFO, he saw a little boy sitting on a bench. Normally, children would run for cover when he appeared because they had no idea what mischief he might be up to.

And Dino saw the opportunity for some fun, so he puffed up his chest and gave a mighty roar.

The little boy didn't run away.

"Why do you do that?" the boy named Simon asked.

Dino was at a loss for words. Then he replied. "Because that's what dinosaurs do!"

"It's rude," Simon said, "And that is why you have no friends."

Dino sat down close to Simon, being careful not to knock him over with his tail.

"What does 'rude' mean?" he asked.

"It means you hurt people's feelings," Simon answered.

So they sat and talked about manners and things that Uncle Sinclair hadn't taught Dino.

"I'm sorry for my past behavior," Dino said. "And I want to have friends to play with."

"Then why don't you follow me to my grandparents' home," Simon offered, "and welcome everyone to their big Christmas tree?"

And so he did, mostly concealed within the tree's branches and wearing a Santa Claus cap to show everyone he was friendly.

He was very surprised when packages were opened that there was a gift for him from the Rinkydinks. It was a laptop computer. (So Dino could communicate better without roaring.)

Which he only does nowadays when the screen goes blank unexpectedly.

This story, written by the Garden Writer, was read on Christmas Eve. I wonder what was given to each Grandchild the next morning.

Snout of Dino

Chapter 34

What the Future Holds

It was one of those quiet fall afternoons, and John and I decided to relax in the old Annsville Hotel for our weekly taping session.

Plato had quietly taken up residence alongside me on the love seat while Pepper dozed at my feet, and John and I talked as two elderly gentlemen who have formed a friendship that will last long after this book is published.

"I wonder if this will still be here twenty years from now," John asked, waving his hands at our surroundings. "You and I," he says, smiling, "won't be. My son wants to come here with his family to live, but I don't see any other folks ready to do what I'm doing. My daughter says she doesn't want any more 'stuff' in her life because she has all she needs."

Pausing to gather his thoughts, he shares, "Ann seldom comes here. I think it's because she thinks this is a 'guy' thing. And in many respects, it is. The other buildings have multiple uses for storage and as a welding shop. So maybe she's right.

"Ann enjoys gardening as much as I do but within the constraints of being a University of California Master Gardener. I do what I want, with no constraints, but with the help and advice of folks with much more regimented lives."

Evidence of that is how he routinely prunes hundreds of roses with power hedge shears, a practice that would give a consulting rosarian screaming fits. But each year, the plants respond with vigorous growth and gorgeous displays of blossoms.

"Living in this place is unlike what visitors see," John says, smiling contentedly. "It's much nicer, honestly. I've got a wife, a home, children, grandchildren, and had a very successful career, and now I have an entirely different situation.

"When I was practicing law, I traveled millions of air miles, surrounded by assistants, and for years, didn't even have my own car. I had drivers to take me where I needed to be. Now most of my traveling is done in our Piglets here on the property."

Ann, it should be noted, retained ownership of her car. And she remains the bookkeeper for the Troll Knoll enterprise, where projects are now talked about in terms of completion, rather than addition.

Life has limits, and so do gardens.

"When a gardener dies, so does their garden" is an oft-repeated phrase. John toyed with the idea of establishing a "garden consortium" of some well-known Northern California gardens whose owners are getting on in years, ultimately using his home as a headquarters for the operation. But there were no takers for the proposal.

"It's possible we could fund Troll Knoll's continued existence," John says with a sigh, "but toward what end? How would anyone, other than a goofy person like me, get the enjoyment out of it?

"I could change some things, I suppose," he concedes, "but what could I do that would make an old geezer happier? I don't know."

As the last page of this book is turned, astute readers who have been to Troll Knoll might comment, "But there's no mention of . . ."

The reason for that is if this chronicle were to keep up with all the innovations and mysteries of Troll Knoll, it would have to be published as a loose-leaf binder. New pages would have to be inserted with every twist and turn of the garden creator's imagination.

For example, there's an idea for a Lewis Carrol pathway along which the Troll might recite passages from *The Walrus and the Carpenter,* including

> "The time has come," the Walrus said, "To talk of many things:
> Of shoes—and ships—and sealing wax—Of cabbages—and kings—
> And why the sea is boiling hot—
> And whether pigs have wings"

Participants on the tour will then notice the presence of winged pigs atop tall posts, answering that question.

Further along, guests will be treated to the Stream of Faces, where nearly forty serene female faces grace the course of a waterway.

Snowcaps on the Coastal Mountains, the volcanic Sutter Buttes and the Valley floor with rivers in the vista

Cast in concrete by John, each colored to match surrounding stones, the closed-eyed faces strongly resemble those found in ancient Buddhist temples. All the faces have a mystic smile, and some blow bubbles from beneath the water.

Still, other guests might notice that the "feet" at the base of floral containers are all left feet. Is there a special meaning?

Not really. When the Troll finds time, casts will be made of a right foot and things will be rectified.

And what about the Train Garden, where a toy from John's childhood days in Mississippi chugs past a sleepy miniature village? It's a work in progress.

Then there's the possibility of Frankenstein's laboratory being assembled near the UFO crash site.

Hmmm.

Time. And good health. Those elements figure so importantly into the creation of the garden.

My prevailing nightmare during the writing of this book was that someday the phone would ring and Ann's voice would be on the other end, saying, "There's been an accident. John was on a tall ladder and . . ."

Men in their seventies, even Trolls, have no business defying gravity and fate. The book would certainly have languished, but more importantly, the wonderful Wednesday mornings we shared, with the boxers in tow, would end.

That didn't happen, and no garden is ever truly "finished." But guests often ask, "Are you content with maintaining the garden as is . . . or are there more attractions on the drawing board?"

The Troll's silent answer is a smile as enigmatic as those on the ladies in the Stream of Faces and a twinkle in his eye.

Thank you very, very much for your interest about Troll Knoll.